THE One and Only SAVIOUR of the WORLD

Carlee Yardley

Ark House Press
PO Box 1722, Port Orchard, WA 98366 USA
PO Box 1321, Mona Vale NSW 1660 Australia
PO Box 318 334, West Harbour, Auckland 0661 New Zealand
arkhousepress.com

© Carlee Yardley 2020

Unless otherwise stated, all Scriptures are taken from the New Living Translation (Holy Bible. New Living Translation copyright© 1996, 2004, 2007, 2013 by Tyndale House Foundation. Used by permission of Tyndale House Publishers Inc., Carol Stream, Illinois 60188. All rights reserved.)

Cataloguing in Publication Data:
Title: The One and Only Saviour of the World
ISBN: 978-0-6488259-3-7 (pbk)
Subjects: Devotional;
Other Authors/Contributors: Yardley, Carlee

Design by initiateagency.com

For my King

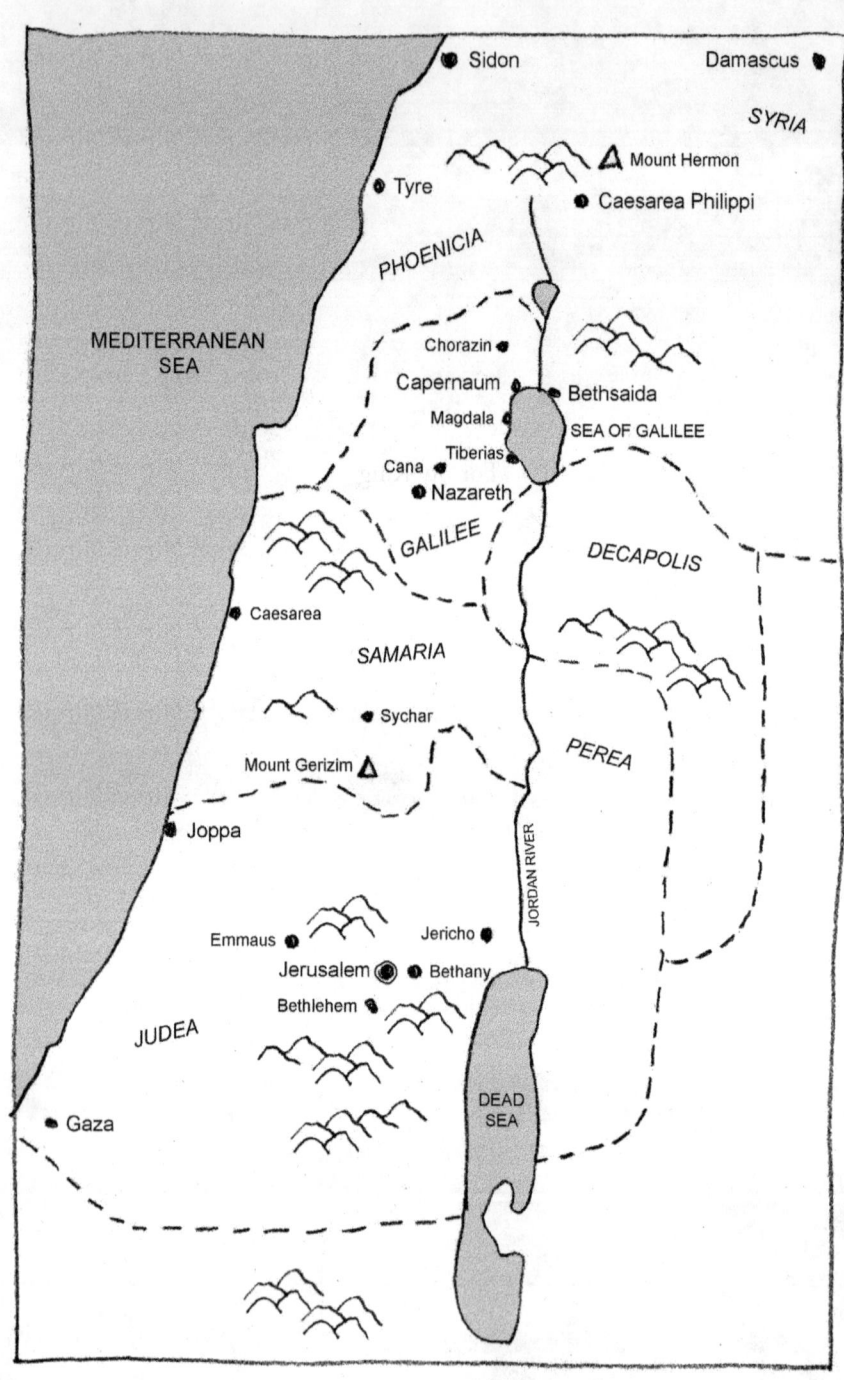

CONTENTS

1. The Eternal Word 1
2. Zechariah and the Angel 2
3. Mary and the Angel 5
4. Joseph and the Angel 7
5. Mary Visits Elizabeth 9
6. The Birth of John the Baptist 11
7. The Birth of Jesus 13
8. The Genealogy of Jesus 16
9. Simeon and Anna 18
10. The Wise Men Find Jesus 20
11. Escape to Egypt 23
12. The Boy at the Temple 25
13. A Voice in the Wilderness 27
14. Jesus is Baptised 31
15. Jesus is Tested 33
16. The Lamb of God 35
17. The First Disciples 37
18. Philip and Nathanael 40
19. The Wedding at Cana 42
20. Jesus Casts Out an Unclean Spirit 44
21. Jesus Heals Many People 46
22. Jesus Preaches in Galilee 48
23. Jesus Rejected at Nazareth 50
24. Jesus Heals a Leper 53

25.	Jesus Heals a Paralysed Man	55
26.	Jesus Calls Matthew	58
27.	A Question About Fasting	60
28.	Jesus Clears the Temple	62
29.	Jesus and Nicodemus	65
30.	John the Baptist Exalts Jesus	68
31.	Jesus and the Samaritan Woman	70
32.	Jesus Heals on the Sabbath	74
33.	God's Chosen Servant	77
34.	The Pool of Bethesda	80
35.	Jesus Claims to be the Son of God	83
36.	The Twelve Apostles	86
37.	The Sermon on the Mount: Beatitudes	89
38.	The Sermon on the Mount: Salt and Light	92
39.	The Sermon on the Mount: Jesus Fulfills the Law	94
40.	The Sermon on the Mount: Anger, Adultery, Divorce and Revenge	96
41.	The Sermon on the Mount: Love your Enemies	98
42.	The Sermon on the Mount: Treasures in Heaven	100
43.	The Sermon on the Mount: Prayer	102
44.	The Sermon on the Mount: Keep Asking, Seeking, Knocking	104
45.	The Sermon on the Mount: Judging Others and Fasting	106
46.	The Sermon on the Mount: The Narrow Gate	108
47.	The Sermon on the Mount: A Tree and its Fruit	109
48.	The Sermon on the Mount: True Disciples	110
49.	The Faith of the Centurion	112
50.	Jesus Raises a Widow's Son	114
51.	Messengers from John the Baptist	116
52.	Judgment on Unbelievers	119

53.	Jesus Anointed by a Sinful Woman	121
54.	Jesus and the Prince of Demons	123
55.	The True Family of Jesus	126
56.	Parable of the Sower	128
57.	Parable of the Wheat and the Weeds	131
58.	The Kingdom of Heaven	133
59.	Jesus Calms the Storm	136
60.	Jesus Heals a Man with a Demon	138
61.	The Bleeding Woman and Jairus' Daughter	140
62.	The Workers Are Few	143
63.	Jesus Sends Out the Twelve Apostles	144
64.	The Death of John the Baptist	148
65.	Jesus Feeds Five Thousand	150
66.	Jesus Walks on Water	152
67.	Many Followers Desert Jesus	154
68.	Inner Purity	158
69.	The Faith of a Gentile Woman	161
70.	Jesus Feeds Four Thousand	163
71.	The Pharisees Demand a Sign	165
72.	The Yeast of the Pharisees and Sadducees	167
73.	Peter's Declaration	169
74.	Jesus Predicts His Death	171
75.	The Transfiguration	173
76.	Jesus Heals a Boy with a Demon	175
77.	Jesus Predicts His Death Again	177
78.	The Temple Tax	179
79.	The Greatest in the Kingdom	181
80.	Using the Name of Jesus	183
81.	Parable of the Unforgiving Servant	185

82.	Marriage and Divorce	187
83.	Jesus Blesses the Children	189
84.	The Rich Young Man	191
85.	Parable of the Vineyard Workers	193
86.	The Festival of Shelters	195
87.	The People Are Divided	198
88.	A Woman Caught in Adultery	200
89.	The People Argue with Jesus	202
90.	Jesus Heals a Man Born Blind	206
91.	Spiritual Blindness	210
92.	The Good Shepherd	212
93.	Jesus Claims to be the Son of God Again	214
94.	Parable of the Good Samaritan	216
95.	Mary and Martha	218
96.	A Warning Against Hypocrisy	220
97.	The Narrow Door	223
98.	Jesus Grieves for Jerusalem	225
99.	A Rebellious Nation	227
100.	Parable of the Rich Fool	229
101.	A Call to Repentance	231
102.	Jesus Heals on the Sabbath	233
103.	Humility	235
104.	A Samaritan Village Rejects Jesus	237
105.	The Cost of Following Jesus	239
106.	Parable of the Lost Sheep and the Lost Coin	241
107.	Parable of the Lost Son	243
108.	Parable of the Dishonest Manager	246
109.	The Rich Man and Lazarus	248
110.	Servanthood	250

111.	Jesus Heals Ten Lepers	251
112.	Parable of the Persistent Widow	253
113.	Parable of the Pharisee and the Tax Collector	255
114.	Jesus Raises Lazarus from the Dead	257
115.	The Plot to Kill Jesus	260
116.	Jesus Predicts His Death a Third Time	262
117.	Greatness is Serving	264
118.	Jesus and Zacchaeus	266
119.	Blind Bartimaeus	268
120.	Parable of the Three Servants	270
121.	The Triumphal Entry	272
122.	Jesus Weeps for Jerusalem	275
123.	Jesus is Anointed at Bethany	277
124.	Jesus Curses the Fig Tree	279
125.	Jesus Clears the Temple Again	281
126.	The Authority of Jesus Challenged	283
127.	Parable of the Evil Farmers	285
128.	The Wedding Banquet	287
129.	The Son of Man Must Be Lifted Up	289
130.	The Unbelief of the People	292
131.	The Leaders Try to Trap Jesus	294
132.	The Greatest Commandment	296
133.	Whose Son is the Messiah?	298
134.	The Widow's Offering	300
135.	The Coming of the Kingdom	302
136.	Parable of the Ten Bridesmaids	306
137.	The Final Judgment	308
138.	Judas and the Plot to Kill Jesus	310
139.	The Last Supper I: Jesus Washes His Disciples' Feet	312

140. The Last Supper II: This is My Body, This is My Blood 315
141. The Last Supper III: Jesus Predicts His Betrayal 317
142. The Last Supper IV: Jesus Predicts Peter's Denial 319
143. The Last Supper V: The Way to the Father 321
144. The Last Supper VI: Jesus Promises the Holy Spirit...................323
145. The Last Supper VII: The Greatest Love and
    The World's Hatred..325
146. The Last Supper VIII: Sadness Will Be Turned to Joy.................328
147. The Last Supper IX: The Prayer of Jesus 331
148. The Garden of Gethsemane 334
149. Jesus is Arrested 337
150. Peter's First Denial 339
151. Jesus Before the High Council 341
152. Peter's Second and Third Denials 344
153. Judas Hangs Himself..346
154. Jesus' Trial Before Pilate 348
155. Jesus Sentenced to Death 351
156. The Crucifixion...355
157. The Death of Jesus 358
158. The Sin-Bearing Messiah...360
159. The Burial of Jesus 363
160. The Resurrection...365
161. The Cover Up 368
162. The Road to Emmaus 370
163. Jesus Appears to his Disciples..372
164. Doubting Thomas...374
165. Jesus Appears in Galilee 376
166. The Great Commission 379

Dear Reader,

I began to write this book after Luke 6:46 hit me in the heart one day. Jesus asked the crowd, "Why do you call me Lord, Lord, but not do what I say?" It was one of those catalyst moments as I realised the obvious: How can we do what he says if we don't know what he says?

In this book you will read my words as I narrate the story, but you need to know that every time Jesus or somebody else speaks, I have taken their words directly from Scripture (NLT). Every word that comes out of Jesus' mouth is life changing and hope giving, and my prayer is that his words will hit you in the heart as you read them, just as they have done for me over and over and over again.

1.

The Eternal Word

John 1:10-13

He came into the very world he created, but the world didn't recognise him. He came to his own people, and even they rejected him. But to all who believed him and accepted him, he gave the right to become children of God. They are reborn - not with a physical birth resulting from human passion or plan, but a birth that comes from God.

2.

Zechariah and the Angel

Luke 1:5-25

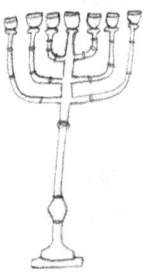

It was the greatest day of Zechariah's life. Of all the priests in his division, he had finally been chosen to burn the incense in the Temple. As he entered the sanctuary, his eyes were wide with reverence. He had dreamed of this moment for so long. Zechariah glanced to his left and ran his eyes along the seven stems of the menorah, the golden lampstand. Never in his life had he seen anything so magnificent. He held his breath as he approached the alter of incense and found himself staring at the veil in front of him. The thick curtain was the only thing separating him from the Most Holy Place, the dwelling place of the Almighty God. Zechariah was suddenly overwhelmed by a crushing feeling of dread and unworthiness, and he looked away quickly. His hands began to tremble as he prepared to light the incense. When he looked up again, the colour drained from his face. There, standing on the right-hand side of the incense alter, was an angel of the Lord. Zechariah's mouth hung open and he stared at the angel in fear. His heart hammered in his chest when the angel spoke.

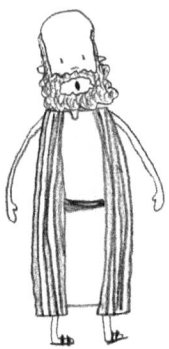

"Don't be afraid, Zechariah! God has heard your prayer. Your wife, Elizabeth, will give you a son, and you are to name him John. You will have great joy and gladness, and many will rejoice at his birth, for he will be great in the eyes of the Lord. He must never touch wine or other alcoholic drinks. He will be filled with the Holy Spirit, even before his birth. And he will turn many Israelites to the Lord their God. He will be a man with the spirit and power of Elijah. He will prepare the people for the coming of the Lord. He will turn the hearts of the fathers to their children, and he will cause those who are rebellious to accept the wisdom of the godly."

Zechariah was frozen in shock. He and his wife, Elizabeth, were always careful to obey God's commandments. They were blameless and righteous in the eyes of God, but everything the angel said was too astonishing to believe! He was an old man, and Elizabeth was an old woman. They had never been able to have children and their hope had fizzled long ago. Zechariah found his voice and asked the angel, "How can I be sure this will happen? I'm an old man now, and my wife is also well along in years."

The angel replied, "I am Gabriel! I stand in the very presence of God. It was he who sent me to bring you this good news! But now, since you didn't believe what I said, you will be silent and unable to speak until the child is born. For my words will certainly be fulfilled at the proper time."

Outside, a great crowd of people had been waiting and praying. It was the custom for the priest to come out and bless them after the incense had been burned, but they were growing restless and were beginning to wonder what was taking so long. When Zechariah finally emerged, his face was as white as a sheet. The people stared at him expectantly, but although his lips were moving, no sound came from them. Zechariah tried to make signs with his hands, and the people realised he must have seen a vision.

When his week of Temple service was over, Zechariah raced home to Elizabeth, and it wasn't long before she was pregnant, just as the angel had said. She kept herself hidden for five months, and praised God for taking away her shame of having no children.

3.

Mary and the Angel

Matthew 1:18, Luke 1:26-38

Not far away, in the village of Nazareth, the angel Gabriel made another surprise visit. This time to Elizabeth's cousin, Mary. Mary gasped as the angel spoke to her.

"Greetings, favoured woman! The Lord is with you!"

Mary stared up at him with eyes full of fear.

"Don't be afraid, Mary," the angel told her, "for you have found favour with God! You will conceive and give birth to a son, and you will name him Jesus. He will be very great and will be called the Son of the Most High. The Lord God will give him the throne of his ancestor David. And he will reign over Israel forever; his Kingdom will never end!"

Mary was terrified and confused. A son? She put her hand on her tummy in wonder, and asked the angel, "But how can this happen? I am a virgin."

The angel replied, "The Holy Spirit will come upon you, and the power of the Most High will overshadow you. So the baby to be born will be holy, and he will be called the Son of God. What's more, your relative Elizabeth has become pregnant in her old age! People used to say she was barren, but she has conceived a son and is now in her sixth month. For the word of God will never fail."

Mary stared at the angel in bewilderment. Nothing he said made sense, but she believed him. She bowed her head as she answered, "I am the Lord's servant. May everything you have said about me come true."

In that moment, Mary laid down her life and trusted God. She knew everything the angel said would cost her dearly. Her reputation would be ruined when everybody realised she was pregnant without a husband. The women in the village would gossip behind her back. They would whisper about the shame she had brought on her family. Tears filled Mary's eyes as she thought of Joseph, her beloved. They were engaged to be married, but Mary wondered how he would react to the news of a baby that wasn't his. Under Jewish law, a woman could be stoned to death for being unfaithful.

Mary's heart beat hard in her chest. She was just a teenager. A humble nobody. But despite her fear, a great sense of awe and courage filled her. She loved God with all her heart and was willing to do whatever he asked of her. Mary closed her eyes and whispered, "Your will be done."

4.

Joseph and the Angel

Matthew 1:19-25

Joseph was shattered. He felt as if his heart was being squeezed right out of his chest. How could Mary do such a thing to him? He loved her more than anything, but he could not marry an unfaithful woman who was carrying somebody else's child. Hurt and confused, he decided to arrange a quiet divorce so Mary would not be publicly humiliated. But before he could make the arrangements, an angel of the Lord appeared to him in a dream.

"Joseph, son of David," the angel said, "do not be afraid to take Mary as your wife. For the child within her was conceived by the Holy Spirit.

And she will have a son, and you are to name him Jesus, for he will save his people from their sins."

Joseph woke with a start. He sat on the end of his bed for a long time with his head in his hands, wrestling with his thoughts and trying to make sense of what the angel had said. Stunned, he remembered the words of the prophet Isaiah:

"Look! The virgin will conceive a child!
    She will give birth to a son,
and they will call him Immanuel,
    which means 'God is with us.'"

Joseph suddenly laughed out loud. He had to find Mary! He raced through the village, his heart bursting with joy knowing now that she hadn't been unfaithful. When he found her, Joseph swept her up and spun her around. He eagerly told Mary about the angel in his dream. They laughed and cried together and marveled at the great thing God was about to do.

5.

Mary Visits Elizabeth

Luke 1:39-56

Mary travelled quickly to a village in the hill country of Judea. When she found the house she was looking for, she called out a greeting. Elizabeth was inside and she cried out in surprise. Her baby had leaped at the sound of Mary's voice, and Elizabeth became filled with the Holy Spirit.

She took Mary's hands and ushered her into the house, exclaiming, "God has blessed you above all women, and your child is blessed. Why am I so honoured, that the mother of my Lord should visit me? When I heard your greeting, the baby in my womb jumped for joy. You are blessed because you believed that the Lord would do what he said."

Mary's eyes shone and her heart felt like it would burst with happiness.

"Oh, how my soul praises the Lord.
>How my spirit rejoices in God my Saviour!

For he took notice of his lowly servant girl,
>and from now on all generations will call me blessed.

For the Mighty One is holy,
>and he has done great things for me.

He shows mercy from generation to generation
>to all who fear him.

His mighty arm has done tremendous things!
>He has scattered the proud and haughty ones.

He has brought down princes from their thrones
>and exalted the humble.

He has filled the hungry with good things
>and sent the rich away with empty hands.

He has helped his servant Israel
>and remembered to be merciful.

For he made this promise to our ancestors,
>to Abraham and his children forever."

For three months Mary stayed with Zechariah and Elizabeth in their home. When it was time for Elizabeth's baby to be born, Mary left them and returned home to Nazareth.

6.

The Birth of John the Baptist

Luke 1:57-80

Elizabeth proudly held her baby as the women fussed over her. Neighbours and relatives had rejoiced when they heard the baby was a boy. Now he was eight days old and they had gathered for his circumcision and naming ceremony.

Everybody assumed the baby's name would be Zechariah, after his father. They stared at Elizabeth in surprise when she told them, "No! His name is John!"

"What?" they exclaimed. "There is no one in all your family by that name."

They turned to Zechariah in confusion and tried to use hand signals to find out what he wanted to call his son. Zechariah gestured for a writing tablet to be brought to him, and on it he wrote four words: "His name is John."

As soon as he finished writing, Zechariah could speak again. He began to laugh, and great tears of happiness rolled down his cheeks. He took the baby gently from Elizabeth, and as he cradled his new son in his hands, he was filled with the Holy Spirit. Zechariah kissed the boy on the forehead and whispered, "You, my little son, will be called the prophet of the Most High, because you will prepare the way for the Lord. You will tell his people how to find salvation through forgiveness of their sins. Because of God's tender mercy, the morning light from heaven is about to break upon us, to give light to those who sit in darkness and in the shadow of death, and to guide us to the path of peace."

News spread quickly throughout the Judean hills and everybody who heard about the baby was in awe. They wondered, "What will this child turn out to be?", for they knew that the hand of the Lord was upon him.

7.

The Birth of Jesus

Luke 2:1-20

Back in Nazareth, Joseph took Mary into his home to be his wife, although he would not sleep with her until after the baby was born. As Mary's pregnancy began to show, Joseph endured the scorn and ridicule that came with it. He pretended not to notice the curious stares as he walked through the marketplace, or the words whispered behind his back.

It was nearly time for the baby to be born when Caesar Augustus, the Roman Emperor, called a census. He wished to count all the people in his vast Empire, which meant every person had to travel to the town of their ancestors to register. Joseph was a direct descendant of the famous King David, so he and Mary had no choice but to make the 144 kilometre journey from Nazareth to Bethlehem, the city of David.

When they arrived in Bethlehem, the small village was crowded with people. Donkeys filled the streets, and children raced about with their cousins. Joseph found the home of a distant relative and he and Mary were enthusiastically welcomed inside. Like every house in Bethlehem, the upstairs living quarters were already filled with guests. There were no spare beds for them, so Mary and Joseph made themselves comfortable downstairs where the animals were brought in each night. It was there that Mary gave birth to a baby boy, just as the angel had told her. She kissed his tiny hands and breathed in his newborn smell. Her heart burst with love as she whispered his name. Jesus. Then she wrapped the baby snugly in strips of cloth and laid him in a manger. Joseph gazed at the boy, so vulnerable and helpless. He watched the rise and fall of his tiny chest and ran his eyes over the tiny crease in his forehead. Tears filled Joseph's eyes. He praised God and quietly wondered what amazing things were in store for the boy.

Out in the hills, a group of shepherds were watching their sheep. The sky was clear, and the village lights glimmered in the distance. Suddenly the hillside around them lit up and an angel of the Lord was there with them. The shepherds huddled together, terrified. But the angel reassured them, "Don't be afraid! I bring you good news that will bring great joy to all people. The Saviour - yes, the Messiah, the Lord - has been born today in Bethlehem, the city of David! And you will recognise him by this sign: You will find a baby wrapped snugly in strips of cloth, lying in a manger."

As he finished speaking, he was joined by hundreds of angels of the heavenly host and they all praised God together.

"Glory to God in highest heaven,
    and peace on earth to those with whom God is pleased."

When the angels had gone back to heaven, the shepherds stood staring into the sky, their mouths hanging wide open. They had never seen such a sight or heard such a glorious sound. As they stood there stunned, they wondered why God would announce his good news to them. They were just lowly shepherds. Humble nobodies who were usually scorned and looked down upon. The men stared at each other, and then with a shout they left their sheep and ran into the village.

The shepherds found Mary and Joseph and were filled with reverence as they knelt before the baby boy. They told Mary what the angel had said on the hillside, and Mary treasured their words and pondered them in her heart. When the shepherds returned to their flocks, they praised and glorified God, and told everybody they met what they had seen.

8.

The Genealogy of Jesus

Matthew 1:1-17, Luke 3:23-38

This is a record of the family tree of Jesus the Messiah. It was prophesied that the Messiah would be a descendant of King David, and through the descendants of Abraham all the nations of the earth would be blessed.

Abraham was the father of Isaac. Isaac was the father of Jacob. Jacob was the father of Judah and his brothers.

Judah was the father of Perez and Zerah. (Their mother was Tamar). Perez was the father of Hezron. Hezron was the father of Aram.

Aram was the father of Amminadab. Amminadab was the father of Nahshon. Nahshon was the father of Salmon.

Salmon was the father of Boaz. (His mother was Rahab). Boaz was the father of Obed. (His mother was Ruth). Obed was the father of Jesse.

Jesse was the father of King David. David was the father of Solomon. (His mother was Bathsheba, the widow of Uriah).

Solomon was the father of Rehoboam. Rehoboam was the father of Abijah. Abijah was the father of Asa.

Asa was the father of Jehoshaphat. Jehoshaphat was the father of Jehoram. Jehoram was the father of Uzziah.

Uzziah was the father of Jotham. Jotham was the father of Ahaz. Ahaz was the father of Hezekiah.

Hezekiah was the father of Manasseh. Manasseh was the father of Amos. Amos was the father of Josiah.

Josiah was the father of Jechoniah and his brothers. (They were born at the time of the exile to Babylon).

After the Babylonian exile: Jechoniah was the father of Shealtiel. Shealtiel was the father of Zerubbabel.

Zerubbabel was the father of Abiud. Abiud was the father of Eliakim. Eliakim was the father of Azor.

Azor was the father of Zadok. Zadok was the father of Achim. Achim was the father of Eliud.

Eliud was the father of Eleazar. Eleazar was the father of Matthan. Matthan was the father of Jacob.

Jacob was the father of Joseph, who was the husband of Mary. Mary was the mother of Jesus Christ the Messiah.

There were fourteen generations from Abraham to David, fourteen from David to the Babylonian exile, and fourteen from the Babylonian exile to Jesus, the Messiah.

9.

Simeon and Anna

Luke 2:21-40

Simeon shuffled across the tiled floor of the Temple courts. He was a righteous old man who was filled with the Holy Spirit. He loved the Lord and had eagerly been waiting for the promised Messiah to come and rescue Israel. God had told him he would not die until he had seen the Messiah with his own eyes.

On that day, the Spirit had led Simeon to the Temple. His eyes jumped from face to face and he studied every person he passed. Mary and Joseph walked through the courts and Simeon watched them closely. There was nothing special about them. They were like hundreds of other parents who came to Jerusalem to present their firstborn sons to the Lord and make the sin offering. But Simeon stared and his heart beat faster. Could it be? Mary clutched the baby to her chest and smiled at the old man as he approached. He stared intently at the baby boy and knew without a doubt that this was the one. Simeon suddenly let out a great laugh and his eyes shone. The Messiah was a baby! Mary and Joseph were amazed as he took Jesus in his arms and praised God, "Sovereign Lord, now let your servant die in peace, as you have promised. I have seen your salvation, which you have prepared for all people.

He is a light to reveal God to the nations, and he is the glory of your people Israel!"

Then Simeon blessed them and told Mary, "This child is destined to cause many in Israel to fall, and many others to rise. He has been sent as a sign from God, but many will oppose him. As a result, the deepest thoughts of many hearts will be revealed. And a sword will pierce your very soul."

Mary's heart thumped as she stared into Simeon's weathered eyes. His words both amazed and frightened her, and she would never forget them.

A prophet named Anna was also at the Temple that day. She was eighty-four years old and her husband had died many years ago. She never left the Temple but stayed there, fasting and praying, and worshipping God day and night. Anna's heart skipped a beat when she saw Simeon holding the baby. She recognised that he was the Messiah, and immediately went and laid her hands on him. Then she began praising God and spreading the news of his birth to anyone who would listen.

Of all the important religious people in the Temple that day, not one of them recognised Jesus, the Saviour of the World. God had chosen only to reveal his Son to two people. Two humble nobodies who loved him with all their hearts and had lived their lives to serve him.

10.

The Wise Men Find Jesus

Matthew 2:1-12

The wise men from the East were full of anticipation as they entered the great city. They had travelled far across the desert, following the star that had finally lead them to Jerusalem. They wasted no time and began asking everybody, "Where is the newborn king of the Jews? We saw his star as it rose, and we have come to worship him."

When King Herod heard what they were saying, he was surprised. A new king? A wave of jealousy swept through him and he was very disturbed. He relished the power and luxury of being king, and it was a well-known fact that he would kill anybody who threatened to take his throne. The news of a new king and challenger made his blood boil.

Herod demanded the leading priests and teachers of religious law be brought to him at once. They were experts of Scripture and would know all the prophecies that referred to the coming Messiah. When they arrived, he exploded in a fit of anger. "Where is the Messiah supposed to be born?"

"In Bethlehem of Judea," they answered nervously, "for this is what the prophet wrote:

'And you, O Bethlehem in the land of Judah,
    are not least among the ruling cities of Judah,
for a ruler will come from you
    who will be the shepherd for my people Israel.'"

The prophet Micah had written those things 700 years earlier.

Herod narrowed his eyes and arranged for the wise men to be brought to him in secret. He asked them the exact time the star had first appeared. When they told him they had seen it around two years earlier, Herod clenched his fists but was careful not to let his anger show. He told the men evenly, "Go to Bethlehem and search carefully for the child. And when you find him, come back and tell me so that I can go and worship him, too!"

As Herod watched them leave the palace, his eyes blazed with resentment and his mind plotted murder.

The star led the wise men ten kilometres from Jerusalem to Bethlehem, to a small house tucked into the hillside. There they found the little king they had been searching for. Mary and Joseph were astounded when the men fell down before Jesus in worship and presented him with expensive gifts of gold, frankincense and myrrh.

When it was time for the wise men to leave Bethlehem, God warned them in a dream to go home a different way and never to return to Herod in Jerusalem.

11.

Escape to Egypt

Matthew 2:13-23

After the wise men left, an angel of the Lord appeared to Joseph in another dream. "Get up! Flee to Egypt with the child and his mother," the angel said. "Stay there until I tell you to return, because Herod is going to search for the child to kill him."

Joseph sat up in terror, his heart racing. He woke Mary and Jesus, and they left their home and all their belongings, and fled to Egypt as refugees.

Meanwhile back in Jerusalem, tension was mounting. The longer Herod waited for the wise men to return, the angrier and more irrational he became. He finally realised they weren't coming back and flew into a fit of rage. Nobody would take his throne. Without knowing exactly where the new king was, Herod ordered the death of every boy in Bethlehem who was aged two years or younger. He had already killed his favourite wife, his mother-in-law and three of his sons, so ordering the death of innocent little boys did not bother his conscience one bit. He would do whatever it took to secure his place on the throne.

At Herod's cruel orders, the soldiers swept through Bethlehem and the surrounding areas, killing all the little boys. Cries of anguish echoed across the hills, and Herod was satisfied.

While his thirst for power was unquenchable, his body was failing. With a long list of medical problems, Herod's life flickered out slowly and painfully. In Egypt, an angel of the Lord appeared to Joseph in another dream. "Get up!" the angel said. "Take the child and his mother back to the land of Israel, because those who were trying to kill the child are dead."

The angel told Joseph to take his family back to the region of Galilee. So they packed up and returned to Nazareth. As they approached the village, their relatives and friends came out to greet the young family. They were home at last.

12.

The Boy at the Temple

Luke 2:41-52

Mary began to panic as she rushed from tent to tent, looking for her son. The Passover Festival had finished, and they had left Jerusalem early that morning to make the three-day journey home to Nazareth. Mary had assumed Jesus was with Joseph or the other boys in their group. But now everywhere she looked, the answer was the same. Nobody had seen him all day.

Joseph was horrified and racked with guilt. He couldn't believe they had left their twelve-year-old son all alone in that big city. Especially at this time of year when Jerusalem was overflowing with pilgrims who had made the journey for the Passover.

Mary and Joseph left their other children with relatives and hurried back the way they had come. Fear cemented itself into Mary's heart as the night grew dark and the campfires that dotted the hillsides burned out one by one. Their tired legs ached, but they hurried on. Finally, as the first rays of sunlight shot up over the hills, they saw the great city sprawled out before them.

They searched the city high and low but could not find Jesus anywhere. On the third day, Mary and Joseph went back to the Temple courts. In one corner, a group of teachers were discussing the Scriptures. A boy sat among them, listening to their words and answering their questions with remarkable understanding. Everybody who heard him was amazed.

When Mary saw him, she burst through the crowd. "Son, why have you done this to us? Your father and I have been frantic, searching for you everywhere."

Jesus stared at his mother. At twelve years old he was on the verge of manhood. He knew he was the Son of God, and he was drawn to the Temple in Jerusalem. He answered Mary, "But why did you need to search? Didn't you know that I must be in my Father's house?"

Mary and Joseph did not understand what he meant, but they hugged him tightly and the three of them left Jerusalem together. Back in Nazareth, Jesus was obedient to his parents and everybody who knew him loved him. He grew in height and in wisdom, and followed Joseph's footsteps in becoming a skilled carpenter. He attended the synagogue, paid his taxes, and waited patiently for God to reveal the moment he would begin his mission.

13.

A Voice in the Wilderness

Matthew 3:1-12, Mark 1:1-8,
Luke 3:1-20, John 1:19-28

Somewhere out in the wilderness, Zechariah's son, John, took a deep breath and picked up his staff. He had received a message from God. It was time. He went down to the Jordan River and began to proclaim, "Repent of your sins and turn to God, for the Kingdom of Heaven is near."

There had not been a prophet in Israel for more than 400 years, so people came from everywhere to hear him. John preached boldly, and told the people that God offers forgiveness to those who are truly sorry for their sin. Peoples' hearts were stirred and one by one they waded into the water and confessed their sins. John baptised each of them as a symbol of their repentance and their commitment to living a new life. Some people became his disciples and stayed with him by the Jordan River.

Over in Jerusalem, Caiaphas, the high priest, heard about John and called the members of the high council together. He wanted to find out why the people were flocking to this strange man, who wore clothes made from camels' hair, and ate locusts with wild honey. They decided that a small band of Pharisees and Sadducees should travel to the Jordan River to spy on John and find out what he was saying to the people. When they arrived, they stood on the bank away from the crowd and watched John closely.

"You brood of vipers!" John suddenly exclaimed. The Pharisees and Sadducees were startled when they realised he was looking straight at them. The men looked around uncomfortably, as John's voice boomed across the riverbank. "Who warned you to flee the coming wrath? Prove by the way you live that you have repented of your sins and turned to God. Don't just say to each other, 'We're safe, for we are descendants of Abraham.' That means nothing, for I tell you, God can create children of Abraham from these very stones. Even now the axe of God's judgment is poised, ready to sever the roots of the trees. Yes, every tree that does not produce good fruit will be chopped down and thrown into the fire.

I baptise with water those who repent of their sins and turn to God. But someone is coming soon who is greater than I am - so much greater that I'm not worthy even to be his slave and carry his sandals. He will baptise you with the Holy Spirit and with fire. He is ready to separate the chaff from the wheat with his winnowing fork. Then he will clean up the threshing area, gathering the wheat into his barn but burning the chaff with never-ending fire."

There was dead silence. Everybody stared at John in disbelief. Nobody spoke to the religious leaders like that and got away with it! The Pharisees and Sadducees were wide eyed, not quite believing what they had just heard.

They firmly believed the Jews were safe from God's judgment because they were his chosen ones. They believed other nations would receive the wrath of God, but the descendants of Abraham would be saved. They had kept their bloodlines pure for that very reason. The Pharisees and Sadducees looked at each other and their eyes flashed angrily. How dare this man speak judgment over them, especially in front of all the common people. But John was not intimidated by them. He would point out evil wherever he saw it, no matter who was offended.

A low murmur went through the crowd and then everybody was talking at once. People called out to John, "What should we do?"

John replied, "If you have two shirts, give one to the poor. If you have food, share it with those who are hungry."

Some corrupt tax collectors were in the crowd. They asked, "Teacher, what should we do?"

John told them, "Collect no more taxes than the government requires."

"And what should we do?" a group of soldiers called.

John replied, "Don't extort money or make false accusations. And be content with your pay."

The Pharisees and Sadducees became enraged as they listened. They had a long list of religious rules and commands that had to be followed. And this hairy man was giving tax collectors and even Gentiles, simple instructions for righteousness! They didn't understand that righteousness is not something that can be earned through deeds. Otherwise it becomes self-righteousness. John knew that true righteousness follows obedience to God, and is demonstrated when we act with integrity and noble character to the people around us. The people in the crowd were in awe, and they began asking John if he was the Messiah, the one who was promised by the prophets. But John shook his head and told them that he wasn't the one.

The Pharisees were shaking with anger by now and they demanded, "Who are you? We need an answer for those who sent us. What do you have to say about yourself?"

The people in the crowd were silent and everybody stared at John in anticipation. His popularity was soaring and the people loved him. John could have chosen that moment to exalt himself. After all, he was a descendant of Aaron and in the priestly line. But it was not about him. Fame and honour weren't important, because he knew God had chosen him for a greater purpose: To prepare the way for the King. He would not point the people to himself, he would only point them to Jesus.

John's eyes blazed and he answered their question with the words of the prophet, Isaiah: "I am a voice shouting in the wilderness, 'Clear the way for the Lord's coming!'"

14.

Jesus is Baptised

Matthew 3:13-17, Mark 1:9-11
Luke 3:21-22, John 1:29-34

John the Baptist stood waist-deep in the Jordan River, baptising the people as they came and boldly preaching his message of repentance. His voice echoed through the valley and the people listened in awe. Suddenly he stopped. His sentence hung in mid-air and he stared. The crowd murmured and strained their necks to follow John's gaze, but all they could see was the lone figure of a man walking slowly down the hillside towards them.

John was silent as the man came closer and closer. When he was finally standing among the crowd, John blinked and called out, "Look! The Lamb of God who takes away the sin of the world! He is the one I was talking about when I said, 'A man is coming after me who is far greater than I am, for he existed long before me.' I did not recognise him as the Messiah, but I have been baptising with water so that he might be revealed to Israel."

Jesus smiled at John. His eyes shone as he waded into the cool water and embraced his cousin. When he asked John to baptise him, John shook his head incredulously. "I am the one who needs to be baptised by you," he said, "so why are you coming to me?"

Jesus replied, "It should be done, for we must carry out all that God requires."

John stared at Jesus for a long moment, then he put his hands on him and lowered him into the water. Jesus came up with water dripping from his beard and his eyes turned towards heaven. At that moment, heaven was torn open and the Spirit of God descended and settled on him like a dove. The people in the crowd stared in awe as a voice came down from heaven, "This is my dearly loved Son, who brings me great joy."

15.

Jesus is Tested

Matthew 4:1-11, Mark 1:12-13, Luke 4:1-13

Jesus was about thirty years old when he left the Jordan River full of the Holy Spirit, and ready to begin his mission. The Spirit led him out into the wilderness, where he stayed for forty days and forty nights without food. The sun beat down on him, flies buzzed around his eyes and Jesus grew weak with hunger.

During that time, Satan came to him and tested him. "If you are the Son of God, tell these stones to become loaves of bread."

Jesus studied the chunks of limestone scattered across the barren ground. His lips were dry and his stomach groaned. He had the power to easily turn those stones to bread, but he looked Satan in the eye and replied, "No! The

Scriptures say, 'People do not live by bread alone, but by every word that comes from the mouth of God.'"

Satan took Jesus to Jerusalem. They stood on the very highest point of the Temple and Satan quoted Scripture back at Jesus. "If you are the Son of God, jump off! For the Scriptures say, 'He will order his angels to protect you. And they will hold you up with their hands so you won't even hurt your foot on a stone.'"

Jesus looked down at the ground far below. He could call on a whole host of angels to catch him and they would come. But instead he replied, "The Scriptures also say, 'You must not test the Lord your God.'"

Next, Satan took Jesus to the top of a very high mountain and showed him all the kingdoms of the world in a moment. "I will give it all to you," he said, "if you will kneel down and worship me."

Jesus looked out across the land. He had watched kingdoms rise and fall as God permitted, since the beginning of time. Satan had no authority over the earth and no power except the power that God allowed him to have.

Weak with hunger and utterly exhausted, Jesus narrowed his eyes. "Get out of here, Satan. For the Scriptures say, 'You must worship the Lord your God and serve only him.'"

As Satan slunk away, angels came and cared for Jesus.

16.

The Lamb of God

John 1:29-42

Jesus left the wilderness and began to head north, to the seaside city of Capernaum. He passed back along the Jordan River, where John the Baptist was standing on the riverbank with two of his disciples. John told the men, "Look! The Lamb of God who takes away the sin of the world! I saw the Holy Spirit descending like a dove from heaven and resting upon him. I didn't know he was the one, but when God sent me to baptise with water, he told me, 'The one on whom you see the Spirit descend and rest is the one who will baptise with the Holy Spirit.' I saw this happen to Jesus, so I testify that he is the Chosen One of God."

The Baptist urged his two disciples to go after Jesus. So they did.

The disciples' names were John and Andrew. They followed Jesus at a distance, but he suddenly turned and waited for them to catch up. Then he asked them, "What do you want?"

The two men were surprised and John replied, "Rabbi (which means 'Teacher'), where are you staying?"

Jesus told them, "Come and see."

So John and Andrew went with Jesus and spent the day with him. When it was time to say goodbye, Andrew raced through Capernaum to find his older brother, Simon. His eyes were wide with excitement and he told him breathlessly, "We have found the Messiah!"

17.

The First Disciples

Matthew 4:18-22,
Mark 1:14-20, Luke 5:1-11

A few days later, Simon and Andrew were mending their nets beside the Sea of Galilee. Andrew worked quickly, eager to join the crowd that was gathering further up the beach. Jesus had begun his preaching ministry and the people had come. They had heard about his baptism and were curious to find out more about him. Andrew strained his ears to hear Jesus' words.

"Repent of your sins and turn to God, for the Kingdom of Heaven is near."

The crowd was growing quickly, and because the people were pushing and jostling one another, Jesus' voice was drowned out. When Andrew looked up from his net again, he was surprised to see Jesus ducking through the crowd and coming towards them. Andrew nodded eagerly when Jesus asked to borrow their boat, and the two brothers pushed him out onto the water. Then they sat down on the shore to listen.

When Jesus had finished preaching, he called Simon over. "Go out where it is deeper, and let down your nets to catch some fish."

Simon looked at Andrew reluctantly. They had been fishing all night and had not caught a thing. He really didn't want to take the boat out again. He had finished his work and was ready to go home to his wife. But Andrew was already gathering up his net, his eyes fixed eagerly on Jesus. Simon sighed, "Master, we worked hard all last night and didn't catch a thing. But if you say so, I'll let the nets down again."

The two brothers went out in the boat and cast the nets where Jesus had said. As they began to pull them up, Simon yelled in surprise. The nets were bulging so full of fish that they began to tear! Andrew shouted for their partners to come and help. John and his older brother James, were busy mending their own nets further down the beach, but they quickly pushed their boat out and helped haul in the catch. Both boats were so full of fish that they were almost sinking.

The four fishermen struggled the catch to shore and then stood bewildered before Jesus.

Jesus studied each of the men and then fixed his eyes on Simon. Simon stared back uncomfortably and his mind raced. He glanced down at the fish spilling out of the nets and suddenly fell to his knees. "Oh, Lord, please leave me - I'm such a sinful man."

But Jesus only looked at him more intently. "Your name is Simon, son of John - but you will be called Cephas" (which means "Peter").

Then Jesus said to the four men standing before him, "Come, follow me, and I will show you how to fish for people!"

Andrew and John leapt forward, ready to follow Jesus wherever he went. Simon, who would be called Peter from that moment on, nodded his head slowly and stepped towards him. Meanwhile, James hadn't taken his eyes off the pile of fish flipping around at his feet. He wondered how his father, Zebedee, would react when he found out they had left his fishing fleet with the hired helpers. James pushed the thought from his mind and wiped his fishy hands on his tunic. He stepped forward with the other men and wondered who Jesus was, and what he could possibly want with four simple fishermen.

The men left their boats and their fish and followed him.

18.

Philip and Nathanael

John 1:43-51

The next day, Jesus and his new disciples walked up to a man named Philip. Jesus said to him, "Come, follow me."

Philip's eyes lit up as he greeted Simon Peter and Andrew. They were childhood friends and had all grown up together in the nearby fishing village of Bethsaida. Then he stared at Jesus. Rumours about him were swirling throughout Galilee, and Philip wondered if what the people were saying about him was true. Could this man really be the Messiah? He studied his friends' earnest faces and knew he had to make a decision.

Philip suddenly asked Jesus to wait there, and then he raced off down the road. He found his friend Nathanael sitting under a fig tree, and told him excitedly, "We have found the very person Moses and the prophets wrote about! His name is Jesus, the son of Joseph from Nazareth."

"Nazareth!" snorted Nathanael, as he got to his feet. "Can anything good come from Nazareth?"

"Come and see for yourself," Philip replied with a smile. He knew he would not convince his friend until he had seen Jesus for himself.

As they hurried back to Jesus, Philip told Nathanael everything he knew about the man. Nathanael was skeptical, but as they approached the group of men, Jesus smiled at him and said, "Now here is a genuine son of Israel - a man of complete integrity."

Nathanael frowned, "How do you know about me?"

Jesus told him, "I could see you under the fig tree before Philip found you."

Nathanael's eyes were wide with surprise, and he exclaimed, "Rabbi, you are the Son of God - the King of Israel!"

Jesus laughed and asked him, "Do you believe this just because I told you I had seen you under the fig tree? You will see greater things than this."

Then he looked at the six men he had chosen to be his disciples. "I tell you the truth, you will all see heaven open and the angels of God going up and down on the Son of Man, the one who is the stairway between heaven and earth."

The men did not know what he meant, but as they followed Jesus, their hearts were full of anticipation.

19.

The Wedding at Cana

John 2:1-12

Jesus and his disciples travelled to Cana for a wedding. Music and laughter burst from the house, and the delicious smell of roasted meat wafted down the street. A few days into the celebration, Jesus' mother, Mary, came to him and whispered urgently, "They have no more wine."

Jesus looked across at the bridegroom's father, who was looking pale and rather anxious. The wedding still had days to go! When the guests realised the wine had run out, the man would be humiliated. Jesus looked down at his mother and kissed her cheek.

"Dear woman, that's not our problem."

Mary continued to stare desperately at him until he laughed. "My time has not yet come."

But Mary had already called the servants over and she told them, "Do whatever he tells you."

Jesus scratched his beard as the servants gathered before him, waiting for instructions. He motioned to six large water jars standing against a wall and said, "Fill the jars with water."

The servants did as he said, and when the jars were filled to the brim, Jesus told them, "Now dip some out, and take it to the master of ceremonies."

The servants looked at each other in shock. They wouldn't dare offer the master of the feast a goblet of water instead of wine! A young servant girl realised there was trouble either way, so she nervously dipped a goblet into the water jar and took it over to the man. The other servants watched anxiously from the other side of the room, and wondered what would happen when the master of the feast realised there was no more wine. They cringed as he put the wine to his lips and then swished it around in his mouth. He suddenly looked surprised and called the bridegroom over. Slapping him on the back, he exclaimed, "A host always serves the best wine first. Then, when everyone has had a lot to drink, he brings out the less expensive wine. But you have kept the best until now!"

He emptied his goblet and yelled for some more.

The servants blinked and stared at Jesus in disbelief. Across the room, Mary's heart raced and she stared in wonder at her son. The wedding celebration went on, and nobody else in the room had any idea of what had just happened.

20.

Jesus Casts Out an Unclean Spirit

Mark 1:21-28, Luke 4:31-37

Jesus returned to Capernaum and began to teach in the synagogue every Sabbath. Everybody who heard him was amazed because he taught with such authority, quite unlike any of the teachers of religious law. One Sabbath day, Jesus was teaching as usual when a man who was possessed by an unclean spirit jumped up. His eyes were wild and he shouted at Jesus, "Why are you interfering with us, Jesus of Nazareth? Have you come to destroy us? I know who you are - the Holy One of God!"

The other people in the synagogue backed away from the man, but Jesus stepped towards him and cut him off. "Be quiet! Come out of the man."

As the people watched, the unclean spirit screamed and threw the man onto the ground. Then it left him. Nobody in the synagogue could believe their eyes and they stared at Jesus in astonishment.

"What sort of new teaching is this?" they asked excitedly. "It has such authority! Even evil spirits obey his orders!"

The people were full of excitement as they left the synagogue, and Jesus' fame spread quickly across the regions surrounding Galilee. Nobody had ever seen anything like this before.

21.

Jesus Heals Many People

Matthew 8:14-17,
Mark 1:29-34, Luke 4:38-41

Back at Simon Peter's house, Peter's mother-in-law was lying in bed with a burning fever. When Jesus arrived, anxious neighbours and relatives surrounded him and begged him to do something. He followed Peter into the room and took the sick woman's hand in his. Then he quietly rebuked the fever, and to Peter's amazement, it left her instantly. Peter stared as she sat up and smiled, then went out to prepare a meal for all the people who had gathered at the house!

News of the miracle spread quickly around the city. When evening came, and the Sabbath day was officially over, a huge crowd came from all around and gathered at Peter's door. They all wanted to see Jesus, and they brought many sick and demon possessed people with them. Excitement rippled through the crowd as Jesus walked among them. Every person he touched was healed and demons were cast out. But Jesus would not let the demons speak because they knew who he was.

22.

Jesus Preaches in Galilee

Matthew 4:23-25,
Mark 1:35-39, Luke 4:42-44

The next morning at daybreak, the crowd gathered back at Simon Peter's house. They waited and waited, and called for Jesus to come out. But Jesus wasn't there. He had left the house while it was still dark to find an isolated place where he could be by himself and pray.

When the people finally realised he wasn't there, they split up and began to look for him. Peter and the other disciples found him first and they told him, "Everyone is looking for you."

The crowd came running and they pressed in around him, begging him to stay. But Jesus told them, "I must preach the Good News of the Kingdom of God in other towns, too, because that is why I was sent."

So Jesus left Capernaum and preached in the synagogues throughout all of Galilee. He was filled with the Holy Spirit and proclaimed the gospel of the Kingdom of God wherever he went. He performed many miracles and his fame spread far and wide, even as far as Syria. The people came from all over Galilee and Judea, even east of the Jordan River, to bring the sick to him. Whatever their sickness or disease was, Jesus healed them all. The demon possessed were set free and the crowds grew. The people exalted Jesus and followed him wherever he went.

23.

Jesus Rejected at Nazareth

Matthew 13:54-58,
Mark 6:1-6, Luke 4:14-30

When Jesus came to his hometown, Nazareth, he went to the synagogue on the Sabbath as usual. Everybody had heard of the miraculous things he had been doing across Galilee and they couldn't take their eyes off him. When the prayers were finished, Jesus was chosen to read from the writings of the prophets. He met the curious stares of his friends and neighbours as he unrolled the scroll that was handed to him. Then he cleared his throat and began to read from the words of Isaiah.

"The Spirit of the Lord is upon me,
    for he has anointed me to bring Good News to the poor.
He has sent me to proclaim that captives will be released,
    that the blind will see,
that the oppressed will be set free,
    and that the time of the Lord's favour has come."

Jesus carefully rolled up the scroll and handed it back to the attendant. Every person in the room was silent and every eye was fixed on Jesus as he sat down. He calculated his next words carefully. They would confirm his mission, but they would also offend the people and turn them against him. Jesus lifted his chin and his voice rang boldly out across the room, "The Scripture you've just heard has been fulfilled this very day!"

Every person in the synagogue was amazed and began speaking at once.

"How can this be?" they asked. "Isn't this Joseph's son?"

"Where did he get all this wisdom and the power to perform such miracles?"

They shook their heads in disbelief. "He's just a carpenter, the son of Mary and the brother of James, Joseph, Judas, and Simon. And his sisters live right here among us."

Jesus sighed as the people continued to mutter and argue about him. Because of their unbelief, he would not give the people of Nazareth any miraculous signs.

The crowd was silenced as Jesus spoke again, "You will undoubtedly quote me this proverb: 'Physician, heal yourself' - meaning, 'Do miracles here in your hometown like those you did in Capernaum.' But I tell you the truth, no prophet is accepted in his own hometown.

Certainly there were many needy widows in Israel in Elijah's time, when the heavens were closed for three and a half years, and a severe famine devastated the land. Yet Elijah was not sent to any of them. He was sent instead to a foreigner - a widow of Zarephath in the land of Sidon. And many in Israel had leprosy in the time of the prophet Elisha, but the only one healed was Naaman, a Syrian."

Jesus' words made the people furious. It was true, in the days of Elijah and Elisha God's grace had extended past the people of Israel and fallen on two foreigners instead. In the same way, Jesus had no obligation to the people of Nazareth. They had no claim to his fame or his miracles. He would offer his grace to whomever he chose, and it would not be them. The crowd was filled with outrage and they rushed towards him. In a mad frenzy they mobbed Jesus and pushed and jostled him out of the village towards some cliffs. They had every intention of throwing him off, but Jesus slipped through the crowd and left the village, unharmed.

24.

Jesus Heals a Leper

Matthew 8:1-4, Mark 1:40-45, Luke 5:12-16

The people in the crowd stepped back in revulsion as the leper came towards them. His clothes were dirty and torn, and the people nearest him began to gag at the smell coming from him. The leper ignored them and searched the crowd frantically with his eyes. When he found Jesus, he fell to the ground with his face in the dust, and begged, "Lord, if you are willing, you can heal me and make me clean."

Jesus looked down at the lonely outcast and was moved with compassion. The law of Moses declared that lepers were unclean, and any unclean person had to live in isolation away from their family and friends. If that wasn't enough, the leper had to draw attention to his status by covering his mouth and calling out, "Unclean! Unclean!" wherever he went. Normally the man would have stayed away from crowds to avoid the humiliation, but he had heard about Jesus and was desperate to meet him.

The crowd stared in horror as Jesus reached out his hand towards the man. It was written that any person who touched a leper, or any object that came into contact with a leper, also became defiled and unclean. But not Jesus. The crowd was about to learn something remarkable about him. Instead of becoming defiled, the opposite would happen. Everything he touched would become clean.

"I am willing," Jesus told the man. "Be healed!"

The man felt Jesus' touch and began to weep uncontrollably. Nobody had touched him in so long. Not since the disease had consumed his body. He stared at the skin on his arms, which was now perfectly smooth. The man clung to Jesus and tears streamed down his face. Jesus instructed him not to tell anyone what had happened. "Go to the priest and let him examine you. Take along the offering required in the law of Moses for those who have been healed of leprosy. This will be a public testimony that you have been cleansed."

But as the man left to find the priest, he forgot Jesus' instructions not to tell anybody. Instead, he spread the news, and everybody who heard was astounded. The crowd following Jesus grew so large that he could no longer enter a town or village or go anywhere in public. So he escaped the people and withdrew into the wilderness to pray and spend time alone with God.

25.

Jesus Heals a Paralysed Man

Matthew 9:1-8, Mark 2:1-12, Luke 5:17-26

When Jesus finally returned to Capernaum, a huge crowd came to see him. Jesus began to teach them, and the crowd grew so thick that the people spilled out of the house and onto the street. Four men arrived carrying their paralysed friend on a mat, and quickly realised they would never get through all those people. But they were desperate and were willing to do anything to get their friend to Jesus. After a short discussion, the four men hauled him up the steep stairs and onto the rooftop.

The people in the house shielded their eyes as pieces of clay and straw began to rain down on them. They watched in surprise as a hole opened up in the ceiling above them, and grew bigger and bigger as the men dug through. When the hole was large enough, the men lowered their paralysed friend right down into the middle of the room! Jesus looked up at the four faces peering through the hole above, and his eyes shone with delight. Seeing their faith, he smiled and said to the paralysed man, "Young man, your sins are forgiven."

Some Pharisees and teachers of religious law were right there in the front row and they frowned and muttered to themselves, "Who does he think he is? That's blasphemy! Only God can forgive sins!"

Every Jew agreed that only God could forgive sins. So when Jesus told the man his sins were forgiven, he was declaring himself equal to God. This was blasphemy, and was a very serious offense. So serious, it could be punished with death by stoning.

Jesus knew what the religious leaders were thinking and he turned to them. "Why do you question this in your hearts? Is it easier to say 'Your sins are forgiven,' or 'Stand up and walk'? So I will prove to you that the Son of Man has the authority on earth to forgive sins."

Jesus turned to the paralysed man and said, "Stand up, pick up your mat, and go home!"

The man's eyes lit up and he jumped up, picked up his mat and pushed his way out of the crowded house. His four friends met him outside and they went away laughing and praising God with all their hearts. The stunned onlookers had never seen anything like it and they also began praising God.

But the religious leaders scowled in annoyance. Everything Jesus said left them puzzled and angry. They firmly believed that if a person had a physical problem it was his own fault and God was punishing him for his sin. But they had just seen with their own eyes that the man had been healed of his disability. That could only mean one thing. God had also forgiven him of his sin. The religious men were trapped by their own beliefs and had no answer. Maybe one day they would understand that Jesus had addressed the more critical thing first. Forgiveness of sin and being made right with God is much more important than any physical need. But for now, the religious leaders could only see one thing: Jesus was threatening their whole religious system every time he spoke.

26.
Jesus Calls Matthew

Matthew 9:9-13,
Mark 2:13-17, Luke 5:27-32

Jesus stood in line with his disciples and waited. His eyes were fixed on Matthew, the tax collector who sat at the booth in front of them. Tax collectors were the most despised of all the Jews. They worked for Rome, collecting taxes from their fellow Jews to send back to the Roman Empire. Everybody knew they collected more taxes than they should and kept the extra for themselves. Tax collectors were extremely wealthy, but the Jews despised them so much, they thought they were no better than murderers and robbers. They were even banned from entering the synagogues.

When it was his turn, Jesus stepped up to Matthew's booth and said, "Follow me and be my disciple."

The other disciples could not believe their ears. A tax collector! John snorted and Simon Peter kicked at the dust uncomfortably. The others watched Matthew warily and hoped he would stay in his seat. They couldn't believe Jesus, a famous rabbi, would want this man that nobody else wanted. He could have chosen anybody to be his disciple. The cleverest man in the synagogue, the richest man, or the most righteous man. But the disciples would soon realise that Jesus doesn't look at people the way the world looks at people. He doesn't choose men who are exceptional on the outside. He chooses them for the potential he can see in their hearts.

Matthew stared at Jesus. Nobody had ever looked at him with eyes full of such love and grace, and the hardness that had built up around his heart fell away. Matthew knew he was a sinner, and in that moment he made a life-changing decision. He stood up and left his booth, giving up everything to follow Jesus.

Matthew immediately began to organise a banquet in his home and invited Jesus to be the guest of honour. When the Pharisees saw what was happening, they were disgusted. Teachers, and people who kept the law, should never share a meal with sinners! They should not even let their clothes touch them.

"Why does your teacher eat with such scum?" they asked the disciples with disdain.

These men believed they were so good and so holy that Jesus could do nothing for them. Matthew on the other hand, knew he was a sinner in trouble, and Jesus could do everything for him. Jesus studied the Pharisee's sour faces and told them, "Healthy people don't need a doctor - sick people do. I have come to call not those who think they are righteous, but those who know they are sinners and need to repent."

27.

A Question About Fasting

Matthew 9:14-17, Mark 2:18-22, Luke 5:33-39

People were beginning to notice that Jesus taught and trained his disciples in a way that was radically different from the other rabbi's. Some people came to him and asked curiously, "John the Baptist's disciples fast and pray regularly, and so do the disciples of the Pharisees. Why are your disciples always eating and drinking?"

Jesus answered, "Do wedding guests fast while celebrating with the groom? Of course not. They can't fast while the groom is with them. But someday the groom will be taken away from them, and then they will fast."

Then Jesus told them two parables. "No one tears a piece of cloth from a new garment and uses it to patch an old garment. For then the new garment would be ruined, and the new patch wouldn't even match the old garment. And no one puts new wine into old wineskins. For the new wine would burst the wineskins, spilling the wine and ruining the skins. New wine must be stored in new wineskins. But no one who drinks the old wine seems to want the new wine. 'The old is just fine,' they say."

The people were silent as they listened to Jesus. The message he was bringing was so shockingly different to anything they knew, it would soon cut their whole idea of religion to the core. The law of Moses had served its purpose and Jesus was about to change everything.

28.

Jesus Clears the Temple

John 2:13-25

Jesus walked slowly around the Temple courts. He had come to Jerusalem for the Passover and his heart was filled with dismay at what he saw. The Temple was supposed to be God's dwelling place on earth. The place where heaven and earth would meet. But instead it had become a marketplace, and business was booming.

Jesus walked over to a pen that was crowded with one-year old lambs. He leant down and ran his hand over their woolly backs. The law stated that any animal offered for sacrifice had to be perfect and unblemished, so the priests charged the people a fee to inspect the animals they brought with them. If an animal was declared unacceptable for sacrifice, the people were forced to purchase one of these lambs from inside the Temple. Jesus frowned as he watched a poor family haggle over a pair of pigeons. All of the animals were overpriced, and the pilgrims who had travelled to Jerusalem were ripped off again and again.

Across the floor, the money changers sat at their tables and counted out coins. Foreign money could not be used to pay the Temple tax or to purchase the animals for sacrifice. So these men took the people's money and exchanged it for Tyrian shekels and half-shekels. The problem was, they did it to their own advantage. They used an unfair exchange rate and always took more money than they gave back. Caiaphas, the high priest, made a profit from every corrupt transaction. His family had become extremely wealthy and the Temple vaults were full of riches.

Jesus clenched his fists in anger. He could not stand by and watch any longer. He breathed out as he picked up some ropes off the ground. Then, without warning, he began swinging them wildly around and around. The disciples watched in alarm as Jesus used the ropes as a whip to drive every animal out of the Temple. Animals ran everywhere and the merchants shouted.

But Jesus was not finished. He strode over to the money changers and threw their tables over. The men yelled furiously as their coins scattered all over the floor and rolled away. Next, Jesus stormed over to the people selling pigeons. He glared at the merchants and bellowed, "Get these things out of here. Stop turning my Father's house into a marketplace!"

He flung the cages open and the pigeons flapped madly across the floor. Everybody in the crowd stared at Jesus in shocked silence. They had never seen such a commotion in the Temple. The Jewish leaders and priests marched towards him, and Jesus met their angry eyes.

Jesus was never angry at sinners who knew they were sinners. No matter what they did or how bad they were, he met them with love and compassion and invited them to change. But he was furious at these self-righteous religious men. The Jewish leaders were supposed to be representing God, but they had twisted God's requirements and used their positions to benefit themselves. They knew all about religion but nothing about the heart of God. God makes it clear that obedience is much more important than performing rituals that don't mean anything. And the Temple had become exactly that. A corrupt and dirty place fueled by empty rituals and meaningless sacrifice.

The Temple priests demanded angrily, "What are you doing? If God gave you authority to do this, show us a miraculous sign to prove it."

Jesus answered them evenly, "Destroy this Temple, and in three days I will raise it up."

The men smirked at one another. "It has taken forty-six years to build this Temple, and you can rebuild it in three days?"

They sneered at Jesus in contempt, but Jesus stood his ground. He wasn't talking about the Temple in Jerusalem. He was referring to his own body.

29.

Jesus and Nicodemus

John 3:1-21

By now, many Pharisees were following Jesus and criticising him loudly wherever he went. So the disciples were surprised one evening when there was a knock at the door and Nicodemus, a well-known Pharisee, was standing outside in the dark.

Nicodemus knew the other Pharisees hated Jesus because he contradicted their teaching, threatened their authority and didn't follow the man-made laws they cherished. But he could not dismiss Jesus so easily. He had heard him preach and had witnessed many of his miracles. There was something about Jesus that touched his heart, and Nicodemus needed to find out more.

When he saw Jesus he said, "Rabbi, we all know that God has sent you to teach us. Your miraculous signs are evidence that God is with you."

Jesus answered, "I tell you the truth, unless you are born again, you cannot see the Kingdom of God."

Nicodemus frowned as he processed Jesus' words.

"What do you mean?" he exclaimed. "How can an old man go back into his mother's womb and be born again?"

Jesus replied, "I assure you, no one can enter the Kingdom of God without being born of water and the Spirit. Humans can reproduce only human life, but the Holy Spirit gives birth to spiritual life. So don't be surprised when I say, 'You must be born again.' The wind blows wherever it wants. Just as you can hear the wind but can't tell where it comes from or where it is going, so you can't explain how people are born of the Spirit."

Nicodemus shook his head. He understood a baby being born with the water from its mother's womb, but he couldn't comprehend what it meant to be born of the Spirit.

"How are these things possible?" he asked.

Jesus replied, "You are a respected Jewish teacher, and yet you don't understand these things?"

He looked Nicodemus square in the eyes. "I assure you, we tell you what we know and have seen, and yet you won't believe our testimony. But if you don't believe me when I tell you about earthly things, how can you possibly believe if I tell you about heavenly things? No one has ever gone to heaven and returned. But the Son of Man has come down from heaven. And as Moses lifted up the bronze snake on a pole in the wilderness, so the Son of Man must be lifted up, so that everyone who believes in him will have eternal life."

Nicodemus knew the Scriptures back to front. His mind raced to the time in the wilderness when God had sent poisonous snakes among the complaining Israelites. Many were bitten and died before the people begged

Moses to ask God to take away the snakes. The Lord had told Moses: "Make a replica of a poisonous snake and attach it to a pole. All who are bitten will live if they simply look at it!"

Nicodemus was perplexed. The people in Moses' day were saved by lifting their eyes to the bronze snake on a pole. But who was the Son of Man? And what did it mean that he would be lifted up?

Jesus gazed at Nicodemus, and his eyes softened. "For this is how God loved the world: He gave his one and only Son, so that everyone who believes in him will not perish but have eternal life. God sent his Son into the world not to judge the world, but to save the world through him."

Nicodemus scratched his head. How he desperately wanted to understand what Jesus meant! If Jesus really was the Son of God, then what did that mean? And could he really offer eternal life? Jesus' next words pierced Nicodemus' heart like tiny arrows.

"There is no judgment against anyone who believes in him. But anyone who does not believe in him has already been judged for not believing in God's one and only Son. And the judgment is based on this fact: God's light came into the world, but people loved the darkness more than the light, for their actions were evil. All who do evil hate the light and refuse to go near it for fear their sins will be exposed. But those who do what is right come to the light so others can see that they are doing what God wants."

Nicodemus left the house with his mind blown. While he didn't understand most of what Jesus had said, something had changed inside him. He wouldn't have been able to explain it to anybody who asked, but a great weight had been lifted from his shoulders. Nicodemus became a secret follower of Jesus that night.

30.

John the Baptist Exalts Jesus

John 3:22-36

John the Baptist had stayed by the Jordan River and was still baptising the people as they came to him. But his disciples were becoming more disgruntled with every day that passed. They had heard that Jesus was preaching throughout Judea and was also baptising people.

One day an argument broke out between John's disciples and some other Jews about ceremonial washing and purification. The disciples went to the Baptist and said, "Rabbi, the man you met on the other side of the Jordan River, the one you identified as the Messiah, is also baptising people. And everybody is going to him instead of coming to us."

John was upset by their comments, and he told his disciples, "No one can receive anything unless God gives it from heaven. You yourselves know how plainly I told you, 'I am not the Messiah. I am only here to prepare the way for him.' It is the bridegroom who marries the bride, and the bridegroom's friend is simply glad to stand with him and hear his vows. Therefore, I am filled with joy at his success."

John paused for a long moment, and then he told them, "He must become greater and greater, and I must become less and less."

His disciples frowned, but John went on, "He has come from above and is greater than anyone else. We are of the earth, and we speak of earthly things, but he has come from heaven and is greater than anyone else. He testifies about what he has seen and heard, but how few believe what he tells them! Anyone who accepts his testimony can affirm that God is true. For he is sent by God. He speaks God's words, for God gives him the Spirit without limit. The Father loves his Son and has put everything into his hands. And anyone who believes in God's Son has eternal life. Anyone who doesn't obey the Son will never experience eternal life but remains under God's angry judgment."

31.

Jesus and the Samaritan Woman

John 4:1-42

It was noon, the hottest part of the day. The Samaritan woman wiped her brow with the back of her hand and laid her water jar in the dirt. Nobody came to the well at this time of day, and that was how she liked it. She was not like the other women from the village, and it was easier to avoid them rather than face their stares and ridicule.

But this time the woman was startled to see a man sitting by the well. She kept her head down as she lowered her jar into the water. When he asked her for a drink, she looked up in surprise.

Firstly, the Jews could not stand the Samaritans and would have nothing to do with them. Secondly, it was not proper for a rabbi to speak to a woman in public. Especially a woman like her. The woman looked at Jesus curiously. She had no idea that he cared more about her than he did about his own reputation.

"You are a Jew, and I am a Samaritan woman. Why are you asking me for a drink?" she asked.

Jesus replied, "If you only knew the gift God has for you and who you are speaking to, you would ask me, and I would give you living water."

The woman frowned. "But sir, you don't have a rope or a bucket, and this well is very deep. Where would you get this living water? And besides, do you think you're greater than our ancestor Jacob, who gave us this well? How can you offer better water than he and his sons and his animals enjoyed?"

Jesus told her, "Anyone who drinks this water will soon become thirsty again. But those who drink the water I give will never be thirsty again. It becomes a fresh, bubbling spring within them, giving them eternal life."

The Samaritan woman looked sideways at Jesus and studied his kind eyes. He spoke to her unlike any man she had ever known. "Please, sir, give me this water! Then I'll never be thirsty again, and I won't have to come here to get water."

Jesus was silent for a moment. Then he challenged her. "Go and get your husband,"

The woman gave him a half smile, "I don't have a husband."

"You're right! You don't have a husband - for you have had five husbands, and you aren't even married to the man you're living with now. You certainly spoke the truth!"

The woman's mouth fell open and she stared at Jesus, shocked that he knew all about her. Then she looked away, her face full of shame. When she looked back at him she was surprised to find no condemnation or judgment in his eyes, only compassion.

"Sir," she said, changing the subject, "you must be a prophet. So tell me, why is it that you Jews insist that Jerusalem is the only place of worship, while we Samaritans claim it is here at Mount Gerizim, where our ancestors worshiped?"

Jesus replied, "Believe me, dear woman, the time is coming when it will no longer matter whether you worship the Father on this mountain or in Jerusalem. You Samaritans know very little about the one you worship, while we Jews know all about him, for salvation comes through the Jews. But the time is coming - indeed it's here now - when true worshipers will worship the Father in spirit and in truth. The Father is looking for those who will worship him that way. For God is Spirit, so those who worship him must worship in spirit and in truth."

The woman frowned, "I know the Messiah is coming - the one who is called Christ. When he comes, he will explain everything to us."

Jesus looked at her intently and told her, "I am the Messiah!"

Jesus had sent his disciples into the village to buy food, and they arrived back at that moment. They were astonished to find him talking to a Samaritan woman, but none of them had the nerve to ask Jesus what they were talking about. The woman suddenly jumped up and rushed back to the village, leaving her water jar behind. She called excitedly to everybody she saw, "Come and see a man who told me everything I ever did! Could he possibly be the Messiah?"

When she was gone, the disciples urged Jesus to eat something. But Jesus told them, "I have a kind of food you know nothing about."

The disciples looked at one another and asked, "Did someone bring him food while we were gone?"

Jesus explained, "My nourishment comes from doing the will of God, who sent me, and from finishing his work. You know the saying, 'Four months between planting and harvest.' But I say, wake up and look around. The fields are already ripe for harvest. The harvesters are paid good wages, and the fruit they harvest is people brought to eternal life. What joy awaits both the planter and the harvester alike! You know the saying, 'One plants and another harvests.' And it's true. I sent you to harvest where you didn't plant; others had already done the work, and now you will get to gather the harvest."

Just then, the Samaritan woman returned with many people from her village. They were eager to meet Jesus and they begged him to stay and teach them. So Jesus stayed in the village of Sychar for two days, teaching and preaching. Many Samaritans heard his message and believed the good news.

They told the woman, "Now we believe, not just because of what you told us, but because we have heard him ourselves. Now we know that he is indeed the Saviour of the world."

32.

Jesus Heals on the Sabbath

Matthew 12:1-14,
Mark 2:23-28, 3:1-6, Luke 6:1-11

One day, the disciples were walking through the fields on the Sabbath, and they began to break off some heads of wheat because they were hungry. They rubbed the wheat between their hands to separate the husks, and chewed the grains as they walked. Some Pharisees had been following them, and when they saw what the disciples were doing, they stopped Jesus in protest. "Look, your disciples are breaking the law by harvesting grain on the Sabbath."

The disciples stopped chewing and looked at Jesus, wondering what he would say. God had clearly instructed the Israelites to work for six days only and rest on the seventh. The Sabbath was supposed to be a good day. A day to rest and enjoy time with one another. But the teachers of religious law, whose job it was to interpret the law, had compiled a list of specific things the people could and could not do on the Sabbath. They had turned it into a burden, a day of rules and regulations. Technically, the disciples had broken the rules, because nobody was allowed to harvest their fields on that day. The Pharisees smirked, fully expecting Jesus to rebuke his men. They couldn't see that they themselves were committing the greater sin, by elevating their man-made traditions above the Word of God.

Jesus ran his hand over the golden wheat as he answered.

"Haven't you read in the Scriptures what David did when he and his companions were hungry? He went into the house of God, and he and his companions broke the law by eating the sacred loaves of bread that only the priests are allowed to eat. And haven't you read in the law of Moses that the priests on duty in the Temple may work on the Sabbath? I tell you, there is one here who is even greater than the Temple! But you would not have condemned my innocent disciples if you knew the meaning of this Scripture: 'I want you to show mercy, not offer sacrifices.' For the Son of Man is Lord, even over the Sabbath!"

They continued on their way, leaving the Pharisees to grumble and moan.

Later that day, Jesus was teaching in the synagogue when he noticed a man with a deformed hand. The teachers of religious law and the Pharisees whispered to one another and watched Jesus closely, eager to have another reason to condemn him. Jesus knew their thoughts, and he motioned to the man with the deformed hand, "Come and stand in front of everyone."

As the man came forward, Jesus looked around the room at the men who were watching him so critically.

"I have a question for you. Does the law permit good deeds on the Sabbath, or is it a day for doing evil? Is this a day to save life or to destroy it?"

He met their accusing eyes one by one, but they were silent and wouldn't answer him. Jesus was annoyed with them, yet sad that their hearts were so hard and unloving. He tried to reason with them. "If you had a sheep that fell into a well on the Sabbath, wouldn't you work to pull it out? Of course you would. And how much more valuable is a person than a sheep! Yes, the law permits a person to do good on the Sabbath."

The teachers of religious law and the stony-faced Pharisees just stared at him with their arms folded. Their rules and their religion were more important to them than the man with the deformed hand. They didn't care about him, but Jesus did. And he would take no notice of made up rules, especially when they excluded love and ignored people in need. He turned to the man, knowing that what he was about to do would set the trigger for his own death sentence. "Hold out your hand."

The man held out his hand, and everybody in the room could see that it was completely normal! Jesus' enemies were furious. They were convinced Jesus was a rogue law breaker who was teaching others to follow his example. They immediately called a meeting and began to discuss plans to kill him.

33.

God's Chosen Servant

Matt 12:15-21

Jesus knew the religious leaders wanted to kill him, so he left the area and moved on. Many people followed, and as he healed the sick among them, he warned them not to tell anybody. He still had many things to do before his mission was accomplished.

Life was difficult for the Jews who lived under Roman rule. Caesar Augustus was the most powerful man in the world and the Roman Empire was thriving. Taxes were high and the Jews had no choice but to pay.

Farmers who couldn't pay their taxes were forced to sell their farms. Some families lost everything and had to beg just to survive.

Most Jews accepted their difficult lives and suffered in silence. Others formed rebellions to fight back, but the Roman army was unbeatable, and the soldiers patrolled the land. Any Jews who rebelled against them were swiftly cut down in short-lived battles.

In all their adversity, the Jewish people clung to the promises of God. They were his chosen people, and just like their ancestors in Egypt, they prayed continually for him to rescue them from their oppressors. The Scriptures were full of prophecies about the coming Messiah. The Saviour King whose reign would never end. The people dreamed of the day when a descendant of King David would restore Israel to glory. When a champion would descend upon the earth and crush their enemies.

There was just one problem. Jesus was the Messiah, but his mission was the exact opposite of what the people were expecting. His purpose was far greater than what they had in mind. Jesus did not come for an earthly battle between kingdoms, and his battle would not be won by the sword. He would not sit on a wooden throne and rule over his people. Instead, he would hang on a cross and die for them. The eternal battle would be won through sacrificial love. He wasn't coming to save the people from their enemies, but he was going to crush the very thing that made them enemies of God. Sin.

Jesus was the One the people were waiting for, but he would not claim his title of Messiah and King until the people understood what that meant.

The prophet Isaiah had lived and written about Jesus seven hundred years earlier:

"Look at my Servant, whom I have chosen.
   He is my Beloved, who pleases me.
I will put my Spirit upon him,
   and he will proclaim justice to the nations.
He will not fight or shout
   or raise his voice in public.
He will not crush the weakest reed
   or put out a flickering candle.
Finally he will cause justice to be victorious.
   And his name will be the hope
     of all the world." (Isaiah 42:1-4)

34.

The Pool of Bethesda

John 5:1-15

Jesus returned to Jerusalem for another Jewish festival. On the Sabbath, he came to the Pool of Bethesda, just inside the city walls, and was confronted with a wretched sight. Bodies of sick people were strewn around the porches surrounding the pool. Some of them were blind, some were lame or paralysed, and many others had diseases that ravaged their bodies. They all gathered there because every so often the water was stirred up and the people believed that the first person into the water would be healed.

Jesus gazed over the porches, his eyes moving from one hopeless person to the next. Some people were close to the water, waiting in anticipation for the first sign of movement. Others stayed back, their eyes dull and lifeless, knowing they had no hope of getting into the pool first. Still others lay curled up in defeat, waiting to die there because they had nowhere else to go.

Jesus' eyes rested on a man laying on the ground nearby. The man was lame and had been that way for thirty-eight years. As Jesus approached, he looked up from his mat and squinted into the sun.

Jesus asked him, "Would you like to get well?"

"I can't, sir," the man replied, "for I have no one to put me into the pool when the water bubbles up. Someone else always gets there ahead of me."

Jesus told him, "Stand up, pick up your mat, and walk!"

At that moment the man was healed, and he stood up in surprise. Then he rolled up his mat and left the pool, looking back at Jesus in awe. When the Jewish leaders saw the man, they stopped him.

"You can't work on the Sabbath! The law doesn't allow you to carry that sleeping mat!"

But the man shrugged and replied, "The man who healed me told me, 'Pick up your mat and walk.'"

The Jewish leaders glanced at one another with narrowed eyes, and demanded, "Who said such a thing as that?"

They were so blinded with hostility that they missed the miracle. A man who had been lame for thirty-eight years was standing right before them completely healed, but all they cared about was their made-up rules and finding out who was breaking them. The man couldn't answer their question, because he didn't know the name of the person who had healed him, and Jesus had already disappeared into the crowd. The leaders scowled and let him go.

Later, Jesus found the same man in the Temple. He told him, "Now you are well; so stop sinning, or something even worse may happen to you."

The man frowned and wondered what could possibly be worse than being unable to walk for thirty-eight years? He was finally off his mat and free to live his life. But Jesus was warning him to keep his eyes on the end goal. Physical sickness lasts only a lifetime. Sin and an unrepentant heart have consequences that last for all eternity.

The man left Jesus and went straight back to the Jewish leaders. When he told them it was Jesus who had healed him, they screwed up their faces in anger, and their hatred towards Jesus intensified. Not only had he broken the Sabbath rules again, he had proven he would not be intimidated by them. It was clear that Jesus would never bow to their demands.

35.

Jesus Claims to be the Son of God

John 5:16-47

The Jewish leaders searched for Jesus and surrounded him with ugly sneers on their faces. They insulted him in front of the crowd and began to persecute him for breaking the Sabbath rules. But Jesus was not moved. He faced them and replied, "My Father is always working, and so am I."

This enraged the leaders. They couldn't believe Jesus had the nerve to call God his Father. Did he really think he was equal to God and his work was as important as God's work? The men murmured angrily among themselves. They had to find a way to kill him before the people began to believe in him.

Their furious eyes locked on Jesus, and he boldly explained, "I tell you the truth, the Son can do nothing by himself. He does only what he sees the Father doing. Whatever the Father does, the Son also does. For the Father loves the Son and shows him everything he is doing. In fact, the Father will show him how to do even greater works than healing this man. Then you will truly be astonished. For just as the Father gives life to those he raises from the dead, so the Son gives life to anyone he wants. In addition, the Father judges no one. Instead, he has given the Son absolute authority to judge, so that everyone will honour the Son, just as they honour the Father. Anyone who does not honour the Son is certainly not honouring the Father who sent him. I tell you the truth, those who listen to my message and believe in God who sent me have eternal life. They will never be condemned for their sins, but they have already passed from death into life. And I assure you that the time is coming, indeed it's here now, when the dead will hear my voice - the voice of the Son of God. And those who listen will live. The Father has life in himself, and he has granted that same life-giving power to his Son. And he has given him authority to judge everyone because he is the Son of Man. Don't be so surprised! Indeed, the time is coming when all the dead in their graves will hear the voice of God's Son, and they will rise again. Those who have done good will rise to experience eternal life, and those who have continued in evil will rise to experience judgment. I can do nothing on my own. I judge as God tells me. Therefore, my judgment is just, because I carry out the will of the one who sent me, not my own will."

The Jewish leaders stared at Jesus, their faces red with rage and their mouths gaping open in horror. But Jesus was not finished. He was not simply a messenger sent from heaven. He was the King himself. Jesus told the men, "You search the Scriptures because you think they give you eternal life. But the Scriptures point to me! Yet you refuse to come to me to receive this life. Your approval means nothing to me, because I know you don't have God's love within you. For I have come to you in my Father's name, and you have rejected me. Yet if others come in their own name, you gladly welcome them. No wonder you can't believe! For you gladly honour each other, but you don't care about the honour that comes from the one who alone is God. Yet it isn't I who will accuse you before the Father. Moses will accuse you! Yes, Moses, in whom you put your hopes. If you really believed Moses, you would believe me, because he wrote about me. But since you don't believe what he wrote, how will you believe what I say?"

Jesus turned and walked away, disappearing into the crowd. The Jewish leaders were left standing there, wide eyed, open mouthed, and completely flabbergasted.

36.

The Twelve Apostles

Matthew 10:1-4, Mark 3:13-19, Luke 6:12-16

By now a large crowd of people followed Jesus and called themselves his disciples. One evening, Jesus left the crowd and went up over the mountainside to pray. He stayed all night long, and in the morning, he called the crowd together to choose twelve men to be his apostles. The crowd listened eagerly as Jesus named them one by one.

Simon Peter was a fisherman from Bethsaida. He was bold and impulsive, and was often the first to speak. He would walk on water in faith, and then moments later sink with doubt. He would chop off a soldier's ear to try and save Jesus, and then deny him three times. In spite of his weaknesses, Simon Peter would become the 'rock', one of the greatest leaders in the early church. He would be killed for preaching about Jesus, and when they crucified him, he would ask to be crucified upside down because he was not worthy of dying in the same way as his Saviour.

Andrew was the brother of Simon Peter and also a fisherman. He was always quick to point others towards Jesus.

James was a fisherman and one of the sons of Zebedee. He and his brother John were nicknamed the 'Sons of Thunder'. James would be the first of the apostles to be martyred, killed for his faith in Jesus.

John was the younger brother of James and also a fisherman. John would become Jesus' closest friend and would refer to himself as "the disciple whom Jesus loved". He would be the only apostle not killed for his faith. Instead he would die of old age in Ephesus, after writing five books of the Bible: The Gospel of John, 1 John, 2 John, 3 John and Revelation.

Philip grew up in Bethsaida, with Simon Peter and Andrew.

Nathanael was also known as Bartholomew, and was a friend of Philips.

Matthew was a tax collector from Capernaum and was also known as Levi. He would write the Gospel of Matthew.

Thomas would become known as 'Doubting Thomas'. He would refuse to believe Jesus had risen from the dead until he had seen Jesus' wounds for himself.

James was the son of Alphaeus, and was also known as the other James, or James the lesser.

Simon was a zealot.

Thaddaeus was also known as Judas.

Judas Iscariot would betray Jesus with a kiss, for thirty pieces of silver. He would then feel devastating remorse for what he had done and take his own life.

These twelve men would walk with Jesus and become his closest friends. He would give them authority to cast out demons and heal every kind of sickness. All of them, except for Judas Iscariot, would take the good news to the nations.

37.

The Sermon on the Mount: Beatitudes

Matthew 5:1-12, Luke 6:20-26

Now that Jesus had chosen the men who would take his message to the world, he began to teach them. Sometimes he taught them while they were alone and other times large crowds listened in. One day, Jesus went up on a mountainside and a whole multitude of people followed him. He sat down and began to preach.

"God blesses those who are poor and realise their need for him,
 for the Kingdom of Heaven is theirs.

God blesses those who mourn,
>   for they will be comforted.
God blesses those who are humble,
>   for they will inherit the whole earth.
God blesses those who hunger and thirst for justice,
>   for they will be satisfied.
God blesses those who are merciful,
>   for they will be shown mercy.
God blesses those whose hearts are pure,
>   for they will see God.
God blesses those who work for peace,
>   for they will be called the children of God.
God blesses those who are persecuted for doing right,
>   for the Kingdom of Heaven is theirs.

"What blessings await you when people hate you and exclude you and mock you and curse you as evil because you follow the Son of Man. When that happens, be happy! Yes, leap for joy! For a great reward awaits you in heaven. And remember, their ancestors treated the ancient prophets that same way.

"What sorrow awaits you who are rich,
>   for you have your only happiness now.
What sorrow awaits you who are fat and prosperous now,
>   for a time of awful hunger awaits you.
What sorrow awaits you who laugh now,
>   for your laughing will turn to mourning and sorrow.
What sorrow awaits you who are praised by the crowds,
>   for their ancestors also praised false prophets."

When Jesus finished speaking, the disciples and the people in the crowd glanced at one another in surprise. They were beginning to believe that Jesus was the Messiah because nobody taught the way he taught or performed the miracles he performed. Jesus had the power to fix their problems with one word. But as they listened, it became clear to them that Jesus hadn't come to fix their immediate problems or fight their battles. He was not sounding like a mighty king who would raise up an army and overthrow the Roman Empire.

Jesus gazed at the people around him. He knew from experience how hard life was under Roman rule. He had worked as a carpenter and helped his mother feed his family. He had seen how the people in his village struggled to pay their taxes. But Jesus knew that fixing the problems wouldn't save the people. It was when they suffered the most, that they realised how little they could do on their own, and how much they needed a Saviour. That's when they would be blessed. Through their hardship they would turn to God and lean on Him. Then they would be saved.

38.

The Sermon on the Mount: Salt and Light

Matthew 5:13-16, Mark 9:49-50,
Luke 11:33-36, 14:34-35

The people in the crowd listened intently as Jesus continued to teach them.

"You are the salt of the earth. But what good is salt if it has lost its flavour? Can you make it salty again? It will be thrown out and trampled underfoot as worthless.

You are the light of the world - like a city on a hilltop that cannot be hidden. No one lights a lamp and then puts it under a basket. Instead, a lamp is placed on a stand, where it gives light to everyone in the house. In the same way, let your good deeds shine out for all to see, so that everyone will praise your heavenly Father."

39.

The Sermon on the Mount: Jesus Fulfills the Law

Matthew 5:17-20, Luke 16:16-17

"Don't misunderstand why I have come. I did not come to abolish the law of Moses or the writings of the prophets. No, I came to accomplish their purpose. I tell you the truth, until heaven and earth disappear, not even the smallest detail of God's law will disappear until its purpose is achieved. So if you ignore the least commandment and teach others to do the same, you will be called the least in the Kingdom of

Heaven. But anyone who obeys God's laws and teaches them will be called great in the Kingdom of Heaven.

But I warn you - unless your righteousness is better than the righteousness of the teachers of religious law and the Pharisees, you will never enter the Kingdom of Heaven!"

40.

The Sermon on the Mount: Anger, Adultery, Divorce and Revenge

Matthew 5:21-42, Luke 16:18

"You have heard that our ancestors were told, 'You must not murder. If you commit murder, you are subject to judgment.' But I say, if you are even angry with someone, you are subject to judgment! If you call someone an idiot, you are in danger of being brought before the court. And if you curse someone, you are in danger of the fires of hell.

So if you are presenting a sacrifice at the altar in the Temple and you suddenly remember that someone has something against you, leave your sacrifice there at the altar. Go and be reconciled to that person. Then come and offer your sacrifice to God.

"You have heard the commandment that says, 'You must not commit adultery.' But I say, anyone who even looks at a woman with lust has already committed adultery with her in his heart. So if your eye - even your good eye - causes you to lust, gouge it out and throw it away. It is better for you to lose one part of your body than for your whole body to be thrown into hell. And if your hand - even your stronger hand - causes you to sin, cut it off and throw it away. It is better for you to lose one part of your body than for your whole body to be thrown into hell.

"You have heard the law that says, 'A man can divorce his wife by merely giving her a written notice of divorce.' But I say that a man who divorces his wife, unless she has been unfaithful, causes her to commit adultery. And anyone who marries a divorced woman also commits adultery.

"You have heard the law that says the punishment must match the injury: 'An eye for an eye, and a tooth for a tooth.' But I say, do not resist an evil person! If someone slaps you on the right cheek, offer the other cheek also. If you are sued in court and your shirt is taken from you, give your coat, too. If a soldier demands that you carry his gear for a mile, carry it two miles. Give to those who ask, and don't turn away from those who want to borrow."

41.

The Sermon on the Mount: Love your Enemies

Matthew 5:43-48, Luke 6:27-36

"You have heard the law that says, 'Love your neighbour' and hate your enemy. But I say, love your enemies! Pray for those who persecute you! In that way, you will be acting as true children of your Father in heaven. For he gives his sunlight to both the evil and the good, and he sends rain on the just and the unjust alike. If you love only those who love you, what reward is there for that? Even corrupt tax collectors do that much. If you are kind only to your friends, how are you different from anyone else? Even pagans do that. But you are to be perfect, even as your Father in heaven is perfect."

The people in the crowd were perplexed. God had given them 613 laws and 10 commandments, and they were hard enough to follow. But now Jesus was setting the bar for righteousness much higher. He was giving them a standard that was impossible to attain, but that was the point. They had to know they were hopeless sinners and could do nothing on their own. The Pharisees thought they were safe by keeping the laws and trying their hardest to look righteous on the outside. But that would never be enough. No matter what they did, their hearts were still ugly and rebellious on the inside.

The people didn't know it yet, but the day was coming when love and holiness would collide. Jesus would live the perfect life they couldn't live and pay the terrible price they couldn't pay. He would take their place, and God would forgive his children without lowering his standards. Anybody who believed would be justified and made righteous by their faith in Jesus Christ alone. Nothing more and nothing less would do.

42.

The Sermon on the Mount: Treasures in Heaven

Matthew 6:1-4, 6:19-34

"Watch out! Don't do your good deeds publicly, to be admired by others, for you will lose the reward from your Father in heaven. When you give to someone in need, don't do as the hypocrites do - blowing trumpets in the synagogues and streets to call attention to their acts of charity! I tell you the truth, they have received all the reward they will ever get. But when you give to someone in need, don't let your left hand know what your right hand is doing. Give your gifts in private, and your Father, who sees everything, will reward you."

"Don't store up treasures here on earth, where moths eat them and rust destroys them, and where thieves break in and steal. Store your treasures in heaven, where moths and rust cannot destroy, and thieves do not break in and steal. Wherever your treasure is, there the desires of your heart will also be."

43.

The Sermon on the Mount: Prayer

Matthew 6:5-15, Luke 11:1-4

"When you pray, don't be like the hypocrites who love to pray publicly on street corners and in the synagogues where everyone can see them. I tell you the truth, that is all the reward they will ever get. But when you pray, go away by yourself, shut the door behind you, and pray to your Father in private. Then your Father, who sees everything, will reward you.

"When you pray, don't babble on and on as the Gentiles do. They think their prayers are answered merely by repeating their words again and again.

Don't be like them, for your Father knows exactly what you need even before you ask him! Pray like this:

> 'Our Father in heaven,
>   may your name be kept holy.
> May your Kingdom come soon.
> May your will be done on earth,
>   as it is in heaven.
> Give us today the food we need,
> and forgive us our sins,
>   as we have forgiven those who sin against us.
> And don't let us yield to temptation,
>   but rescue us from the evil one.'

"If you forgive those who sin against you, your heavenly Father will forgive you. But if you refuse to forgive others, your Father will not forgive your sins."

44.

The Sermon on the Mount: Keep Asking, Seeking, Knocking

Matthew 7:7-12, Luke 11:5-13

"Suppose you went to a friend's house at midnight, wanting to borrow three loaves of bread. You say to him, 'A friend of mine has just arrived for a visit, and I have nothing for him to eat.' And suppose he calls out from his bedroom, 'Don't bother me. The door is locked for the night, and my family and I are all in bed. I can't help you.' But I tell you this - though he won't do it for friendship's sake, if you keep knocking long enough, he will get up and give you whatever you need because of your shameless persistence.

"And so I tell you, keep on asking, and you will receive what you ask for. Keep on seeking, and you will find. Keep on knocking, and the door will be opened to you. For everyone who asks, receives. Everyone who seeks, finds. And to everyone who knocks, the door will be opened.

"You fathers - if your children ask for a fish, do you give them a snake instead? Or if they ask for an egg, do you give them a scorpion? Of course not! So if you sinful people know how to give good gifts to your children, how much more will your heavenly Father give the Holy Spirit to those who ask him."

45.
The Sermon on the Mount: Judging Others and Fasting

Matthew 6:16-18, 7:1-6, Luke 6:37-42

"Do not judge others, and you will not be judged. For you will be treated as you treat others. The standard you use in judging is the standard by which you will be judged. And why worry about a speck in your friend's eye when you have a log in your own? How can you think of saying to your friend, 'Let me help you get rid of that speck in your eye,' when you can't see past the log in your own eye? Hypocrite! First get rid of the log in your own eye; then you will see well enough to deal with the speck in your friend's eye.

"Don't waste what is holy on people who are unholy. Don't throw your pearls to pigs! They will trample the pearls, then turn and attack you.

"And when you fast, don't make it obvious, as the hypocrites do, for they try to look miserable and dishevelled so people will admire them for their fasting. I tell you the truth, that is the only reward they will ever get. But when you fast, comb your hair and wash your face. Then no one will notice that you are fasting, except your Father, who knows what you do in private. And your Father, who sees everything, will reward you."

46.

The Sermon on the Mount: The Narrow Gate

Matthew 7:13-14

"You can enter God's Kingdom only through the narrow gate. The highway to hell is broad, and its gate is wide for the many who choose that way. But the gateway to life is very narrow and the road is difficult, and only a few ever find it."

47.

The Sermon on the Mount: A Tree and its Fruit

Matthew 7:15-20, Luke 6:43-45

"Beware of false prophets who come disguised as harmless sheep but are really vicious wolves. You can identify them by their fruit, that is, by the way they act. Can you pick grapes from thornbushes, or figs from thistles? A good tree produces good fruit, and a bad tree produces bad fruit. A good tree can't produce bad fruit, and a bad tree can't produce good fruit. So every tree that does not produce good fruit is chopped down and thrown into the fire. Yes, just as you can identify a tree by its fruit, so you can identify people by their actions. A good person produces good things from the treasury of a good heart, and an evil person produces evil things from the treasury of an evil heart. What you say flows from what is in your heart."

48.

The Sermon on the Mount: True Disciples

Matthew 7:21-29, Luke 6:46-49, 13:22-30

"Not everyone who calls out to me, 'Lord! Lord!' will enter the Kingdom of Heaven. Only those who actually do the will of my Father in heaven will enter. On judgment day many will say to me, 'Lord! Lord! We prophesied in your name and cast out demons in your name and performed many miracles in your name.' But I will reply, 'I never knew you. Get away from me, you who break God's laws.'"

Jesus scanned the faces in the crowd. He knew that many people would claim to follow him without ever truly meeting him. Those people needed to know the truth, even if it was hard to hear. Because knowing his name would not be enough. Even the demons knew his name. To find him interesting would not be enough. To study him and try to be like him would not be enough. To memorise the Scriptures, to keep the rules and to act the right way would never be enough. Anybody who made a decision to follow Jesus but then kept on sinning without a care, had not really chosen to follow him at all. True followers would be eager to obey him, because if you love your king, you do what he says.

Jesus sighed. "So why do you keep calling me 'Lord, Lord!' when you don't do what I say? Anyone who listens to my teaching and follows it is wise, like a person who builds a house on solid rock. Though the rain comes in torrents and the floodwaters rise and the winds beat against that house, it won't collapse because it is built on bedrock. But anyone who hears my teaching and doesn't obey it is foolish, like a person who builds a house on sand. When the rains and floods come and the winds beat against that house, it will collapse with a mighty crash."

Everybody who heard Jesus was amazed at everything he said, because they had never heard anybody speak with such authority.

49.

The Faith of the Centurion

Matthew 8:5-13, Luke 7:1-10

Back in Capernaum, an anxious Roman centurion paced backwards and forwards. He had a servant who was very dear to him, and the servant was dying. The centurion had heard about Jesus, and had asked some respected Jewish leaders to go to him and ask if he would heal the man.

When the leaders found Jesus they pleaded earnestly with him. "If anyone deserves your help, he does, for he loves the Jewish people and even built a synagogue for us."

The Jewish leaders thought the centurion was worthy of Jesus' help because of what he had done for the Jews. They didn't understand that Jesus helps anybody who asks. His grace does not have to be earned and it can never be bought.

Jesus went with the leaders, but before they arrived at the house, the centurion met them along the road. He said to Jesus, "Lord, don't trouble yourself by coming to my home, for I am not worthy of such an honour. I am not even worthy to come and meet you. Just say the word from where you are, and my servant will be healed. I know this because I am under the authority of my superior officers, and I have authority over my soldiers. I only need to say, 'Go,' and they go, or 'Come,' and they come. And if I say to my slaves, 'Do this,' they do it."

Jesus listened in amazement, then he put his arm around the centurion's shoulders and turned to the large crowd that had been following him. "I tell you the truth, I haven't seen faith like this in all Israel! And I tell you this, that many Gentiles will come from all over the world - from east and west - and sit down with Abraham, Isaac, and Jacob at the feast in the Kingdom of Heaven. But many Israelites - those for whom the Kingdom was prepared - will be thrown into outer darkness, where there will be weeping and gnashing of teeth."

The Jewish leaders narrowed their eyes at him, but Jesus smiled at the centurion, "Go back home. Because you believed, it has happened."

His servant was healed at that very moment.

50.

Jesus Raises a Widow's Son

Luke 7:11-17

A large crowd was following Jesus as he approached the town of Nain. At the gates, they all stood aside to make way for a funeral procession that was coming out of the town. Jesus' eyes locked on a distraught woman who was being supported by the other mourners. She was already a widow and now her only son had died. Her life would be very difficult because she no longer had a husband or children to provide for her and care for her as she grew old.

Great tears of anguish streamed down the woman's face and she stumbled after her dead son. As Jesus watched her, his heart overflowed with compassion. He stepped towards the woman and told her not to cry. Then he walked over to the open coffin and touched it.

"Young man," he said, "I tell you, get up."

The woman stared in amazement as her son sat up and began to talk to the people around him. Jesus gave him to his mother and new tears of joy spilled down her cheeks as she kissed his face over and over again.

The people in the crowd stared in awe and fear swept over them. All at once they began to praise God, saying, "A mighty prophet has risen among us," and "God has visited his people today."

The report of this miracle spread all over Judea and even further.

51.
Messengers from John the Baptist

Matthew 11:1-19, Luke 7:18-35

John the Baptist stared at the small square of light near the roof of his cell. His back ached and the stones of the prison walls felt cold against his body. His bold preaching had come to an end after he publicly condemned Herod Antipas for being married to his brother's wife, Herodias. Herodias had been furious and wanted to kill the Baptist, but

Herod refused because he knew John was a good and holy man. To appease his wife, Herod had thrown John into prison, but he made sure he was protected while he was there.

Whenever John's disciples came to the prison to visit, they told him all about the amazing things Jesus was doing. In the long, lonely hours that followed, John would dwell on their words and wonder. He was sure Jesus was the one they were expecting. The Scriptures had foretold all the things the Messiah would do, and Jesus was doing them all. But John still wondered, and he longed to hear Jesus confirm it himself. One day John sent two of his disciples to ask Jesus, "Are you the Messiah we've been expecting, or should we keep looking for someone else?"

Then he leaned his head back against the cold stones and waited.

When John's disciples found Jesus, they told him, "John the Baptist sent us to ask, 'Are you the one who is to come, or should we look for someone else?'".

Jesus looked intently at the men, and told them, "Go back to John and tell him what you have heard and seen - the blind see, the lame walk, those with leprosy are cured, the deaf hear, the dead are raised to life, and the Good News is being preached to the poor."

Then he added, "God blesses those who do not fall away because of me."

Jesus watched the men walk away to report to John, and his heart grew heavy. He turned to the crowd and asked them, "What kind of man did you go into the wilderness to see? Was he a weak reed, swayed by every breath of wind? Or were you expecting to see a man dressed in expensive clothes? No, people with expensive clothes live in palaces. Were you looking for a prophet? Yes, and he is more than a prophet. John is the man to whom the Scriptures refer when they say,

> 'Look, I am sending my messenger ahead of you,
>   and he will prepare your way before you.'

"I tell you the truth, of all who have ever lived, none is greater than John the Baptist. Yet even the least person in the Kingdom of Heaven is greater than he is! And from the time John the Baptist began preaching until now, the Kingdom of Heaven has been forcefully advancing, and violent people are attacking it. For before John came, all the prophets and the law of Moses looked forward to this present time. And if you are willing to accept what I say, he is Elijah, the one the prophets said would come. Anyone with ears to hear should listen and understand!"

Many people in the crowd had been baptised by John and they nodded in agreement. But the Pharisees and the experts of religious law only scowled. They had rejected John's offer to be baptised and had therefore rejected God's plan for redemption.

Jesus frowned and looked into their faces. He and John had preached the same message of hope, with completely different methods, yet the religious men were determined to be offended by both of them.

Jesus sighed, "To what can I compare the people of this generation? How can I describe them? They are like children playing a game in the public square. They complain to their friends,

'We played wedding songs,
    and you didn't dance,
so we played funeral songs,
    and you didn't weep.'

"For John the Baptist didn't spend his time eating bread or drinking wine, and you say, 'He's possessed by a demon.' The Son of Man, on the other hand, feasts and drinks, and you say, 'He's a glutton and a drunkard, and a friend of tax collectors and other sinners!' But wisdom is shown to be right by the lives of those who follow it."

52.

Judgment on Unbelievers

Matthew 11:20-30, Luke 10:13-15, 10:21-24

Jesus had performed many miracles in the cities of Chorazin, Bethsaida and Capernaum, but the people in those cities could not see beyond the amazing things Jesus could do for them. They could not see that Jesus was offering them more than just miracles. He was offering them the greatest gift of grace: forgiveness of their sin and eternal life with their Father in heaven. But the people didn't want to change, and they refused to turn from their sin and turn to God.

Jesus warned them, "What sorrow awaits you, Chorazin and Bethsaida! For if the miracles I did in you had been done in wicked Tyre and Sidon, their people would have repented of their sins long ago, clothing themselves in burlap and throwing ashes on their heads to show their remorse. I tell you, Tyre and Sidon will be better off on judgment day than you.

And you people of Capernaum, will you be honoured in heaven? No, you will go down to the place of the dead. For if the miracles I did for you had been done in wicked Sodom, it would still be here today. I tell you, even Sodom will be better off on judgment day than you."

The people should have been shocked by Jesus' words. In the days of Abraham and Lot, fire and burning sulfur had rained down on the city of Sodom, destroying everything in it. God had poured out his judgment on the Sodomites who were proud, gluttonous and lazy. They had done detestable things and ignored the poor who suffered right outside their doors. But the people of Capernaum ignored Jesus and his warnings and went about their business. Their indifference to him would put them in the same place as the people of Sodom.

Jesus looked to heaven and prayed out loud, "O Father, Lord of heaven and earth, thank you for hiding these things from those who think themselves wise and clever, and for revealing them to the childlike. Yes, Father, it pleased you to do it this way! My Father has entrusted everything to me. No one truly knows the Son except the Father, and no one truly knows the Father except the Son and those to whom the Son chooses to reveal him."

Then Jesus turned to those in the crowd who did believe his message and would choose to follow him. His eyes softened and he told them gently, "Come to me, all of you who are weary and carry heavy burdens, and I will give you rest. Take my yoke upon you. Let me teach you, because I am humble and gentle at heart, and you will find rest for your souls. For my yoke is easy to bear, and the burden I give you is light."

53.

Jesus Anointed by a Sinful Woman

Luke 7:36-50

A Pharisee named Simon invited Jesus to his home for a meal. As Jesus reclined at the table, a woman slipped nervously into the room. Her heart was pounding in her chest and she kept her head down. The guests stared at her and wondered what in the world she was doing there. She was painfully aware of the silence that fell across the room as she knelt behind Jesus and cracked open a beautiful alabaster jar. As she poured the expensive perfume from the jar onto his feet, her face burned with shame and she began to weep. The woman knew she was a sinner and her heart was filled with grief at the things she had done. She kissed Jesus' feet and used her hair to wipe her tears from them.

Simon, the host, recognised what sort of woman she was and scowled in disgust. He thought to himself, "If this man were a prophet, he would know what kind of woman is touching him. She's a sinner!"

Jesus looked Simon in the eyes and said, "Simon, I have something to say to you. A man loaned money to two people - 500 pieces of silver to one and 50 pieces to the other. But neither of them could repay him, so he kindly forgave them both, canceling their debts. Who do you suppose loved him more after that?"

Simon answered, "I suppose the one for whom he canceled the larger debt."

"That's right," Jesus said. Then he motioned to the woman. "Look at this woman kneeling here. When I entered your home, you didn't offer me water to wash the dust from my feet, but she has washed them with her tears and wiped them with her hair. You didn't greet me with a kiss, but from the time I first came in, she has not stopped kissing my feet. You neglected the courtesy of olive oil to anoint my head, but she has anointed my feet with rare perfume. I tell you, her sins - and they are many - have been forgiven, so she has shown me much love. But a person who is forgiven little shows only little love."

The woman lifted her eyes to meet his. She knew she was unworthy, a hopeless sinner in need of a Saviour. She also knew there was nothing she could do but fall at the feet of Jesus. And that's what made her worthy.

Jesus smiled at the woman and told her gently, "Your sins are forgiven."

The men sitting around the table shook their heads and muttered angrily, "Who is this man, that he goes around forgiving sins?"

Sadly, they missed three things. They missed Jesus' words of grace and salvation, because they were too busy being offended. Secondly, they missed their own sin, because they were too busy judging the woman's. But most importantly, they missed the moment a sinful nobody was allowed to anoint the King of kings.

Jesus helped the woman up. "Your faith has saved you; go in peace."

54.

Jesus and the Prince of Demons

Matthew 12:22-37,
Mark 3:20-30, Luke 11:14-28

Crowds formed everywhere Jesus went. Sometimes he and his disciples could not even find the time to eat. On one such day, a large crowd of people brought a demon possessed man to Jesus. The man was blind and couldn't speak, but when Jesus touched him, he fell to his knees and stared wide eyed at everyone around him. He could see! Tears ran down his cheeks and he began to speak for the first time.

The people in the crowd were amazed, and they wondered out loud, "Could it be that Jesus is the Son of David, the Messiah?"

Some Pharisees overheard what the people were saying and they scoffed, "He's possessed by Satan, the prince of demons. That's where he gets the power to cast out demons."

Jesus knew their thoughts and turned on them. "How can Satan cast out Satan? Any kingdom divided by civil war is doomed. A town or family splintered by feuding will fall apart. And if Satan is casting out Satan, he is divided and fighting against himself. His own kingdom will not survive. And if I am empowered by Satan, what about your own exorcists? They cast out demons, too, so they will condemn you for what you have said. But if I am casting out demons by the Spirit of God, then the Kingdom of God has arrived among you. For who is powerful enough to enter the house of a strong man and plunder his goods? Only someone even stronger - someone who could tie him up and then plunder his house."

The Pharisees glowered at Jesus in contempt, but they had no reply. Jesus' heart grew heavy as he gazed at them. These men claimed to love God, but most of them were arrogant, self-righteous and critical. They knew Scripture back to front, but their hearts were as hard as stone.

Jesus groaned. "Anyone who isn't with me opposes me, and anyone who isn't working with me is actually working against me. So I tell you, every sin and blasphemy can be forgiven - except blasphemy against the Holy Spirit, which will never be forgiven. Anyone who speaks against the Son of Man can be forgiven, but anyone who speaks against the Holy Spirit will never be forgiven, either in this world or in the world to come. A tree is identified by its fruit. If a tree is good, its fruit will be good. If a tree is bad, its fruit will be bad."

Jesus paused and his voice cracked. "You brood of snakes! How could evil men like you speak what is good and right? For whatever is in your heart determines what you say. A good person produces good things from the treasury of a good heart, and an evil person produces evil things from the treasury of an evil heart. And I tell you this, you must give an account on judgment day for every idle word you speak. The words you say will either acquit you or condemn you."

The Pharisees spat on the ground and Jesus watched them walk away.

55.
The True Family of Jesus

Matthew 12:46-50,
Mark 3:31-35, Luke 8:19-21

Jesus' mother, Mary, and his four brothers were standing out in the crowd. His brothers - James, Joseph, Simon and Judas - had listened in dismay as the people wondered if Jesus could be the promised Messiah. They didn't yet believe in him and they were shocked at the way Jesus spoke to the Pharisees.

"He's out of his mind," the brothers whispered to one another. They tried to get Jesus' attention so they could take him home, but the crowd was thick and they could not get near him. When Jesus went into the house, they sent somebody to tell him, "Your mother and your brothers are standing outside, and they want to speak to you."

Jesus asked, "Who is my mother? Who are my brothers?"

He gazed around the room and his eyes met those of the men and women who were seated around him. They had walked with him faithfully, day after day. Jesus stretched out his hand towards them and said, "Look, these are my mother and brothers. Anyone who does the will of my Father in heaven is my brother and sister and mother!"

56.

Parable of the Sower

Matthew 13:1-23, Mark 4:1-20, Luke 8:1-15

The teachers of religious law and the Pharisees were now watching every move Jesus made. Wherever he went, they were there with critical eyes and sneering lips. Jesus stopped teaching in the synagogues and instead began to teach out in the open air. A large group of men and women followed him and supported him with their own money. Among them was a woman named Susanna, and a woman named Joanna, who was the wife of Chuza, Herod's household manager. Mary Magdalene was also there. Jesus had cast seven demons from her and now she followed him wherever he went.

One day, Jesus was sitting beside the sea when a large crowd of people gathered, eager to hear him preach. He got into a boat and went out onto the water so everyone could hear him.

"Listen! A farmer went out to plant some seeds. As he scattered them across his field, some seeds fell on a footpath, and the birds came and ate them. Other seeds fell on shallow soil with underlying rock. The seeds sprouted quickly because the soil was shallow. But the plants soon wilted under the hot sun, and since they didn't have deep roots, they died. Other seeds fell among thorns that grew up and choked out the tender plants. Still other seeds fell on fertile soil, and they produced a crop that was thirty, sixty, and even a hundred times as much as had been planted! Anyone with ears to hear should listen and understand."

Later, when the disciples were alone with Jesus, they asked him, "Why do you use parables when you talk to the people?"

Jesus explained to them, "You are permitted to understand the secrets of the Kingdom of Heaven, but others are not. To those who listen to my teaching, more understanding will be given, and they will have an abundance of knowledge. But for those who are not listening, even what little understanding they have will be taken away from them. That is why I use these parables,

'For they look, but they don't really see.
They hear, but they don't really listen or understand.'

This fulfills the prophecy of Isaiah that says,

'When you hear what I say,
   you will not understand.
When you see what I do,
   you will not comprehend.
For the hearts of these people are hardened,
   and their ears cannot hear,
and they have closed their eyes -
   so their eyes cannot see,
and their ears cannot hear,
   and their hearts cannot understand,
and they cannot turn to me
   and let me heal them.'

"But blessed are your eyes, because they see; and your ears, because they hear. I tell you the truth, many prophets and righteous people longed to see what you see, but they didn't see it. And they longed to hear what you hear, but they didn't hear it."

The disciples leaned in as Jesus explained the parable about the farmer planting seeds. "The seed that fell on the footpath represents those who hear the message about the Kingdom and don't understand it. Then the evil one comes and snatches away the seed that was planted in their hearts. The seed on the rocky soil represents those who hear the message and immediately receive it with joy. But since they don't have deep roots, they don't last long. They fall away as soon as they have problems or are persecuted for believing God's word. The seed that fell among the thorns represents those who hear God's word, but all too quickly the message is crowded out by the worries of this life and the lure of wealth, so no fruit is produced. The seed that fell on good soil represents those who truly hear and understand God's word and produce a harvest of thirty, sixty, or even a hundred times as much as had been planted!"

57.

Parable of the Wheat and the Weeds

Matthew 13:24-30, 13:36-43

Jesus told another parable. "The Kingdom of Heaven is like a farmer who planted good seed in his field. But that night as the workers slept, his enemy came and planted weeds among the wheat, then slipped away. When the crop began to grow and produce grain, the weeds also grew. The farmer's workers went to him and said, 'Sir, the field where you planted that good seed is full of weeds! Where did they come from?'

'An enemy has done this!' the farmer exclaimed.

'Should we pull out the weeds?' they asked.

'No,' he replied, 'you'll uproot the wheat if you do. Let both grow together until the harvest. Then I will tell the harvesters to sort out the weeds, tie them into bundles, and burn them, and to put the wheat in the barn.'"

When they were alone with Jesus again, the disciples asked him, "Please explain to us the story of the weeds in the field."

So Jesus told them, "The Son of Man is the farmer who plants the good seed. The field is the world, and the good seed represents the people of the Kingdom. The weeds are the people who belong to the evil one. The enemy who planted the weeds among the wheat is the devil. The harvest is the end of the world, and the harvesters are the angels.

Just as the weeds are sorted out and burned in the fire, so it will be at the end of the world. The Son of Man will send his angels, and they will remove from his Kingdom everything that causes sin and all who do evil. And the angels will throw them into the fiery furnace, where there will be weeping and gnashing of teeth. Then the righteous will shine like the sun in their Father's Kingdom. Anyone with ears to hear should listen and understand!"

58.

The Kingdom of Heaven

Matthew 13:31-35, 13:44-52,
Mark 4:21-34, Luke 13:16-21

Seven hundred years before Jesus was born, the prophet Isaiah had written about him:

"I will speak to you in parables.
  I will explain things hidden since the creation of the world."

Some of Jesus' parables were easy to understand. Others were not, and Jesus explained them to his disciples once they were alone.

"What is the Kingdom of God like? How can I illustrate it? It is like a mustard seed planted in the ground. It is the smallest of all seeds, but it becomes the largest of all garden plants; it grows long branches, and birds can make nests in its shade.

"What else is the Kingdom of God like? It is like the yeast a woman used in making bread. Even though she put only a little yeast in three measures of flour, it permeated every part of the dough.

"The Kingdom of Heaven is like a treasure that a man discovered hidden in a field. In his excitement, he hid it again and sold everything he owned to get enough money to buy the field.

"Again, the Kingdom of Heaven is like a merchant on the lookout for choice pearls. When he discovered a pearl of great value, he sold everything he owned and bought it!

"Again, the Kingdom of Heaven is like a fishing net that was thrown into the water and caught fish of every kind. When the net was full, they dragged it up onto the shore, sat down, and sorted the good fish into crates, but threw the bad ones away. That is the way it will be at the end of the world. The angels will come and separate the wicked people from the righteous, throwing the wicked into the fiery furnace, where there will be weeping and gnashing of teeth.

"No one lights a lamp and then covers it with a bowl or hides it under a bed. A lamp is placed on a stand, where its light can be seen by all who enter the house. For everything that is hidden will eventually be brought into the open, and every secret will be brought to light. Anyone with ears to hear should listen and understand.

"The Kingdom of God is like a farmer who scatters seed on the ground. Night and day, while he's asleep or awake, the seed sprouts and grows, but he does not understand how it happens. The earth produces the crops on its own. First a leaf blade pushes through, then the heads of wheat are formed, and finally the grain ripens. And as soon as the grain is ready, the farmer comes and harvests it with a sickle, for the harvest time has come."

When Jesus had told many parables, he asked his disciples, "Do you understand all these things?"

When they said yes, he told them, "Every teacher of religious law who becomes a disciple in the Kingdom of Heaven is like a homeowner who brings from his storeroom new gems of truth as well as old."

59.

Jesus Calms the Storm

Matthew 8:23-27,
Mark 4:35-41, Luke 8:22-25

One day, as evening was approaching, Jesus asked his disciples to take him across the sea to the other side. He was exhausted as he got into the boat and was asleep within minutes.

The disciples kept a steady rhythm as they rowed and talked quietly about the things Jesus had done. The lame had walked, the blind had seen, and the dead had come alive. They shared story after story and none of them noticed the storm rolling in.

The soft breeze suddenly became a fierce, howling gale. The men on the oars strained to keep their course as the sea spray hit their faces. James took charge and ordered the other disciples to secure everything in the boat and prepare to ride out the storm.

James and John braced themselves against the mast and their eyes met in alarm. They had spent most of their lives fishing on the Sea of Galilee, and they knew how quickly conditions could change. The wind would rush down the ravines from the mountain tops, turning the water into a churning, raging mess in minutes. The brothers had been caught in hundreds of storms, but this was surely one of the worst.

The boat was thrown around violently as the waves rose up and then crashed down onto the deck. The men scrambled over one another, desperate to find something to hold on to. The disciples looked for Jesus and were amazed that he could still be asleep. Somebody yelled for him, and the others joined in.

"Lord, save us! We're going to drown!"

Jesus sat up and looked at the frightened men, whose eyes were wide with terror. "Why are you afraid? You have so little faith!"

John realised at once that he had cried out in desperation for his life, not in faith that Jesus could save him. His heart sank and he stared at Jesus. Then he clenched his teeth as another wave battered the boat, sending a wall of water crashing over them all.

Jesus stood up and rebuked the wind and the waves. His voice boomed over the roar of the storm. "Silence! Be still!"

At once there was a great calm. The sea was flat. The air was still. And the men lay on the deck, staring into the clear dark sky. Their hearts hammered in their chests and they were filled with awe and amazement. "Who is this man?" they asked one another. "Even the wind and waves obey him!"

60.
Jesus Heals a Man with a Demon

Matthew 8:28-34,
Mark 5:1-20, Luke 8:26-39

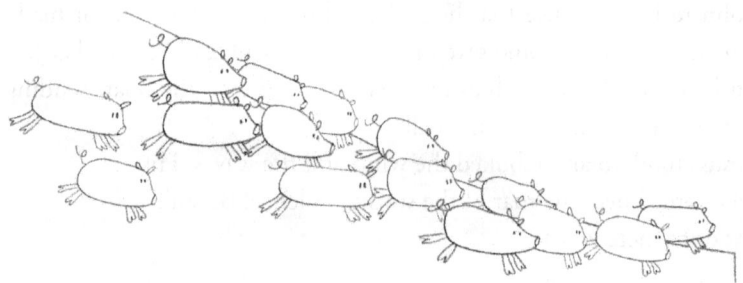

When they arrived at the other side of the sea, they were in the region of the Gerasenes. As Jesus stepped onto the shore, blood curdling screams filled the air. A demon possessed man ran and threw himself at Jesus' feet, shrieking loudly. The man was naked and had been living among the tombs in the hillside for years. People from the town had tried to bind him with chains, but each time they did, he snapped the chains like they were made of paper. Then he ran out into the wilderness under the control of the demons. Day and night the man wandered through the hills, screaming and cutting himself with sharp stones. He was so violent that nobody would go anywhere near him.

Jesus looked intently at the man and commanded the evil spirit to come out. But he screamed, "Why are you interfering with me, Jesus, Son of the Most High God? Please, I beg you, don't torture me!"

"What is your name?" Jesus asked him.

"My name is Legion, because there are many of us inside this man."

The demons begged Jesus not to send them into the abyss, the bottomless pit. A large herd of pigs was feeding on the hillside nearby, and the demons begged Jesus to let them enter the pigs instead. Jesus gave them permission and the demons immediately left the man. At that moment, the whole herd of two thousand pigs ran down the hill, plunged into the sea and drowned.

The herdsmen who had been watching the pigs were horrified. They fled to the nearby towns and spread the news of what had happened. A large crowd came running, and they stared in disbelief at the man who had been demon possessed. He was now fully clothed and sitting calmly at Jesus' feet. All of the people were terrified and they pleaded with Jesus to leave them alone.

As Jesus got into the boat to leave, the man begged to go with him. But Jesus sent him away. "No, go back to your family, and tell them everything God has done for you."

So the man left Jesus and went all through the town, telling everybody what had happened to him. Everybody who heard was amazed.

61.
The Bleeding Woman and Jairus' Daughter

Matthew 9:18-26,
Mark 5:21-43, Luke 8:40-56

Jesus crossed back to the other side of the sea, where a large crowd of people had been waiting for him. A man named Jairus pushed to the front of the crowd. He was the leader of the local synagogue, and he fell to his knees and begged Jesus to come to his house. His only daughter, who was twelve years old, was dying. Jesus went with Jairus and the crowd swarmed after them.

There was a woman at the edge of the crowd who had been bleeding for twelve years. She had spent all her money on doctors, but nobody could make the bleeding stop. The law said that when a woman was bleeding she was unclean. Anything she touched or sat on became unclean, and if she had contact with another person, they would also become unclean. The woman had been a lonely outcast for twelve years.

She was too ashamed to approach Jesus, but she thought to herself, "If I can just touch his robe, I will be healed."

The woman pushed her way through the crowd, closer and closer to Jesus.

She was almost close enough to touch him, when the crowd surged forwards and sent her off balance. She tripped and stumbled, scraping her hands and knees on the gravel. Jesus was about to disappear through the crowd, so the woman lunged forward in desperation and her fingers brushed the fringe of Jesus' robe. At that very moment she felt the bleeding stop and she knew instantly that she had been healed.

Jesus stopped walking and turned around. The woman froze as he asked the crowd, "Who touched me?"

The disciples were confused. Simon Peter said, "Master, this whole crowd is pressing up against you."

But Jesus told him, "Someone deliberately touched me, for I felt healing power go out from me."

The woman began to tremble when she realised Jesus knew. In that terrifying moment, she understood that Jesus always, without fail, notices every person who reaches out to him. Knowing she could not stay hidden, she came to him and fell at his feet. The crowd listened and her face burned with shame as she told him why she had touched him. Jesus took her trembling hands and helped her to her feet. He smiled warmly and said, "Daughter, your faith has made you well. Go in peace. Your suffering is over."

While Jesus was still speaking to the woman, a messenger arrived and spoke quietly to Jairus. "Your daughter is dead. There's no use troubling the Teacher now."

Jairus' face crumpled in grief, but Jesus told him, "Don't be afraid. Just have faith, and she will be healed."

When they got to Jairus' house, they were met with a huge commotion. People wailed and wept, and bitter funeral music filled the house. Jesus told all the people, "Get out! The girl isn't dead; she's only asleep."

They all laughed at him, because they knew she had died.

Jesus sent everybody away from the house, except for Simon Peter, James, and John. They went into the room where the girl was laying, and Jesus took her small hand in his. "Little girl, get up!"

At once the girl's life returned. She opened her eyes and Jairus and his wife began to weep with joy. Jesus told them to give her something to eat, and not to tell anyone what had happened. But the report of the miracle spread far and wide across the whole countryside.

62.

The Workers Are Few

Matthew 9:35-38

Everywhere Jesus went, his heart broke for those who were suffering. Many had serious illnesses and disabilities, and many more were hungry and couldn't pay their taxes. On the fringe of every crowd, Jesus saw rejects and lonely outcasts, people overwhelmed with never-ending problems. He had compassion on them because they were helpless and lost, like sheep without a shepherd. But when he looked at them, he saw past their hopelessness. He saw precious gems, people made in the image of God. People made for a purpose and people in need of a Saviour.

Jesus turned to his disciples and told them, "The harvest is great, but the workers are few. So pray to the Lord who is in charge of the harvest; ask him to send more workers into his fields."

63.

Jesus Sends Out the Twelve Apostles

Matthew 10:5-42, Mark 6:7-13, 13:9-13,
Luke 9:1-6, 10:1-20, 12:4-12, 12:49-53

Jesus called his twelve disciples together and told them he was sending them out to proclaim the Kingdom of God. They would go in pairs, and he would give them the power to heal the sick and the authority to cast out demons. The twelve men listened intently as Jesus gave them their final instructions.

"Don't go to the Gentiles or the Samaritans, but only to the people of Israel - God's lost sheep. Go and announce to them that the Kingdom of

Heaven is near. Heal the sick, raise the dead, cure those with leprosy, and cast out demons. Give as freely as you have received!

"Don't take any money in your money belts - no gold, silver, or even copper coins. Don't carry a traveller's bag with a change of clothes and sandals or even a walking stick. Don't hesitate to accept hospitality, because those who work deserve to be fed.

"If any household or town refuses to welcome you or listen to your message, shake its dust from your feet as you leave. I tell you the truth, the wicked cities of Sodom and Gomorrah will be better off than such a town on the judgment day.

"Look, I am sending you out as sheep among wolves. So be as shrewd as snakes and harmless as doves. But beware! For you will be handed over to the courts and will be flogged with whips in the synagogues. You will stand trial before governors and kings because you are my followers. But this will be your opportunity to tell the rulers and other unbelievers about me. When you are arrested, don't worry about how to respond or what to say. God will give you the right words at the right time. For it is not you who will be speaking - it will be the Spirit of your Father speaking through you.

"A brother will betray his brother to death, a father will betray his own child, and children will rebel against their parents and cause them to be killed. And all nations will hate you because you are my followers. But everyone who endures to the end will be saved. When you are persecuted in one town, flee to the next. I tell you the truth, the Son of Man will return before you have reached all the towns of Israel.

"Students are not greater than their teacher, and slaves are not greater than their master. Students are to be like their teacher, and slaves are to be like their master. And since I, the master of the household, have been called the prince of demons, the members of my household will be called by even worse names!

"But don't be afraid of those who threaten you. For the time is coming when everything that is covered will be revealed, and all that is secret will be made known to all. What I tell you now in the darkness, shout abroad when daybreak comes. What I whisper in your ear, shout from the housetops for all to hear!

"Don't be afraid of those who want to kill your body; they cannot touch your soul. Fear only God, who can destroy both soul and body in hell. What is the price of two sparrows - one copper coin? But not a single sparrow can fall to the ground without your Father knowing it. And the very hairs on your head are all numbered. So don't be afraid; you are more valuable to God than a whole flock of sparrows.

"Everyone who acknowledges me publicly here on earth, I will also acknowledge before my Father in heaven. But everyone who denies me here on earth, I will also deny before my Father in heaven.

"I have come to set the world on fire, and I wish it were already burning! I have a terrible baptism of suffering ahead of me, and I am under a heavy burden until it is accomplished.

"Don't imagine that I came to bring peace to the earth! I came not to bring peace, but a sword. From now on families will be split apart, three in favour of me, and two against - or two in favour and three against.

'Father will be divided against son
   and son against father;
mother against daughter
   and daughter against mother;
and mother-in-law against daughter-in-law
   and daughter-in-law against mother-in-law.
Your enemies will be right in your own household!'

"If you love your father or mother more than you love me, you are not worthy of being mine; or if you love your son or daughter more than me, you are not worthy of being mine. If you refuse to take up your cross and follow me, you are not worthy of being mine. If you cling to your life, you will lose it; but if you give up your life for me, you will find it.

"Anyone who receives you receives me, and anyone who receives me receives the Father who sent me."

After Jesus finished speaking, the apostles went boldly out, two by two. They were welcomed into many towns and chased from many others. People heard and joyfully accepted the good news, while others rejected it. The apostles healed the sick and cast out demons, then they returned to Jesus and excitedly told him everything they had done in his name.

64.

The Death of John the Baptist

Matthew 14:3-12, Mark 6:17-29

King Herod laughed and clapped his hands in delight as his daughter danced. It was his birthday and he had thrown a grand party for himself. The banquet hall was full of important guests and everybody was having a good time. When the music stopped, Herod called his daughter over. He was so pleased with her performance, and so drunk on wine, that he said loudly, "Ask me for anything you like, and I will give it to you."

His lips stretched into a wide, satisfied smile and he vowed in front of all his guests, "I will give you whatever you ask, up to half my kingdom!"

The girl left the hall and ran straight to her mother to ask what her request should be. Her mother, Herodias, smirked with pleasure. She knew exactly what she wanted. Revenge. She told her daughter, "Ask for the head of John the Baptist!"

Herodias watched smugly as her daughter ran back to Herod with her request. The blood drained from Herod's face and he was immediately sorry he had made such a foolish oath. But his guests were watching him expectantly and he knew he could not go back on his word in front of them. He reluctantly sent an executioner to the prison, and it wasn't long before the man returned with John's head on a tray. It was presented to the girl, who took it straight to her triumphant mother.

When John the Baptist's disciples heard what had happened, they collected his body and buried it in a tomb. John's mission on earth had come to an end, but this courageous and humble man would always be known as a man who lived, and died, only to point people to Jesus.

65.

Jesus Feeds Five Thousand

Matthew 14:13-21, Mark 6:30-46,
Luke 9:10-17, John 6:1-15

A messenger came early the next morning to tell Jesus the news of the Baptist's death. Jesus' shoulders sagged and he immediately got into the boat with his disciples. They left the crowds behind and found a secluded place in the hills near Bethsaida, where they could be alone in their grief. But the people anticipated where they were going and ran ahead to meet them. Jesus' heart ached and he was tired, but when he saw the people climbing the hills to get to him, he was filled with compassion.

He healed the sick among them and taught them many things about the Kingdom of God.

Late in the afternoon the disciples interrupted him. "This is a remote place, and it's already getting late. Send the crowds away so they can go to the nearby farms and villages and buy something to eat."

But Jesus answered, "You feed them."

He turned to Philip and asked, "Where can we buy bread to feed all these people?"

Of course Jesus didn't need Philip or anyone else to solve the problem. He already knew what he was going to do, but he asked Philip the question to test him.

Philip frowned, "Even if we worked for months, we wouldn't have enough money to feed them!"

Then Andrew spoke up. "There's a young boy here with five barley loaves and two fish. But what good is that with this huge crowd?"

Jesus smiled as he crouched down in front of the boy. The boy knew he didn't have much, but he was willing to give it all to Jesus. His eyes lit up as Jesus took the five loaves and two fish and instructed the crowd to sit in groups of fifty or so. There were five thousand men, and many more women and children sitting on the hill.

Jesus took the loaves and looked to heaven. He gave thanks to God and broke the bread into pieces. Then the disciples began to pass the bread out until everybody had some. Jesus did the same with the fish, and the people ate and ate. When everybody was full, the disciples collected twelve baskets of leftovers.

Everybody was amazed by this miracle and began talking excitedly amongst themselves. "Surely, he is the Prophet we have been expecting!"

Jesus knew the people were about to take him and force him to be their king, so he sent his disciples back to the boat and told them to go on ahead to Capernaum. Then he withdrew from the crowd and went higher up into the hills by himself to pray.

66.

Jesus Walks on Water

Matthew 14:22-33,
Mark 6:47-52, John 6:16-21

It had been a long day, and the disciples were exhausted as they got into the boat without Jesus and headed for Capernaum. They struggled with the oars well into the night, because the waves were battering the boat and a strong headwind blew against them. In the early hours of the morning, they were only about six kilometres from where they had started, and Matthew yelled in terror. There, walking towards them on the water, was the figure of a man. The disciples thought he was a ghost and they clung to one another in fear.

But the man called out, "Don't be afraid. I am here!"

They knew that voice well, and they stared at the man in confusion. Simon Peter gathered his courage and called out shakily, "Lord, if it's really you, tell me to come to you, walking on the water."

"Yes, come," Jesus replied.

Peter looked at Jesus across the inky water and slowly climbed out of the boat. With a deep breath he took a tentative step. Then he took another and suddenly he was walking on the water! The other disciples watched in awe and began to shout encouragement. Peter laughed nervously. He was getting bolder with each step. But suddenly he took his eyes off Jesus and looked down. The water looked cold and frightening and Peter's eyes grew wide. He looked wildly around at the waves and felt the wind blowing against him. Suddenly aware of the danger around him, Peter's courage faltered. As he panicked, he began to sink.

"Save me, Lord!" he shouted.

Jesus immediately reached out and grabbed Peter's hand. "You have so little faith," he said. "Why did you doubt me?"

They climbed into the boat together, and all at once the wind stopped. The disciples began to talk excitedly and they worshipped Jesus, saying, "You really are the Son of God!"

67.

Many Followers Desert Jesus

John 6:22-71

The next morning, the crowd gathered back on the shore. They had seen the disciples leave in the boat without Jesus, and they expected him to come down from the hills at any moment. Several boats from Tiberias came and landed on the shore, but when the people finally realised Jesus was not coming back, they got into the boats and headed for Capernaum to look for him.

When they found Jesus there, they asked him, "Rabbi, when did you get here?"

Jesus knew their hearts and said, "I tell you the truth, you want to be with me because I fed you, not because you understood the miraculous signs. But don't be so concerned about perishable things like food. Spend your energy seeking the eternal life that the Son of Man can give you. For God the Father has given me the seal of his approval."

The people replied, "We want to perform God's works, too. What should we do?"

Jesus told them, "This is the only work God wants from you: Believe in the one he has sent."

The people were not impressed by this answer. "Show us a miraculous sign if you want us to believe in you. What can you do?"

Behind Jesus, Simon Peter snorted. These were the same fickle people who had just been fed with five loaves and two fish!

They ignored Peter and continued, "After all, our ancestors ate manna while they journeyed through the wilderness! The Scriptures say, 'Moses gave them bread from heaven to eat.'"

Jesus replied, "I tell you the truth, Moses didn't give you bread from heaven. My Father did. And now he offers you the true bread from heaven. The true bread of God is the one who comes down from heaven and gives life to the world."

"Sir," they said, "give us that bread every day."

The people were eager for another free lunch. They wanted to make Jesus their king because he had fed them and showed them miraculous power. Jesus sighed. He wanted nothing to do with the earthly kingdom they had in mind. His Kingdom would be everlasting and far greater than anything they could ever dream of. The people in his Kingdom would be truly satisfied forever.

"I am the bread of life. Whoever comes to me will never be hungry again. Whoever believes in me will never be thirsty. But you haven't believed in me even though you have seen me."

The people murmured and argued among themselves. "Isn't this Jesus, the son of Joseph? We know his father and mother. How can he say, 'I came down from heaven'?"

They frowned as they looked Jesus up and down. This plain, poor carpenter certainly could not be the Messiah they were expecting! They began to argue again, but Jesus interrupted them, "Stop complaining about what

I said. For no one can come to me unless the Father who sent me draws them to me, and at the last day I will raise them up. I tell you the truth, anyone who believes has eternal life. Yes, I am the bread of life! Your ancestors ate manna in the wilderness, but they all died. Anyone who eats the bread from heaven, however, will never die. I am the living bread that came down from heaven. Anyone who eats this bread will live forever; and this bread, which I will offer so the world may live, is my flesh."

The people stared dumbly at Jesus. "How can this man give us his flesh to eat?"

Jesus said it again. "I tell you the truth, unless you eat the flesh of the Son of Man and drink his blood, you cannot have eternal life within you. But anyone who eats my flesh and drinks my blood has eternal life, and I will raise that person at the last day. For my flesh is true food, and my blood is true drink. Anyone who eats my flesh and drinks my blood remains in me, and I in him. I live because of the living Father who sent me; in the same way, anyone who feeds on me will live because of me."

Jesus' disciples looked awkwardly around the crowd. Even they were disturbed and unsure of what Jesus was saying. They asked themselves, "This is very hard to understand. How can anyone accept it?"

Jesus knew what his disciples were thinking. He turned to them and asked, "Does this offend you? Then what will you think if you see the Son of Man ascend to heaven again? The Spirit alone gives eternal life. Human effort accomplishes nothing. And the very words I have spoken to you are spirit and life. But some of you do not believe me."

Simon Peter stared at Jesus in bewilderment. John and the others looked down at the ground. The people in the crowd began to turn away. One by one they left Jesus, shaking their heads as they walked away. Jesus' heart ached for them, but he was not surprised. He knew there would always be people who followed him because of his popularity, his miracles and the free food. They would lose interest as soon as something better caught their eye. Many others would slip away as soon as he talked about sacrifice and self-denial. They were the ones who wanted the benefits of a Saviour but were not willing to surrender their lives to him. So, Jesus let them go. He was looking for people with sincere hearts. People who were hungry for the truth. People who were bold enough to follow him and stand with him all the way to the cross.

Jesus turned to his twelve men and motioned to the disappearing crowd. "Are you also going to leave?"

Simon Peter answered for them all. "Lord, to whom would we go? You have the words that give eternal life. We believe, and we know you are the Holy One of God."

68.

Inner Purity

Matthew 15:1-20, Mark 7:1-23

One day a group of Pharisees and teachers of religious law came all the way from Jerusalem to meet Jesus. They noticed right away that some of his disciples didn't perform the hand washing ritual. The religious men were stunned, and they asked Jesus, "Why do your disciples disobey our age-old tradition? For they ignore our tradition of ceremonial hand washing before they eat."

Jesus studied them carefully. The hand washing they were talking about had little to do with germs or hygiene. It was a ritual that the teachers of religious law had invented to cleanse the hands in case they had touched anything unclean without realising it. If the hands were washed in a certain way, then the food they were about to touch would not be defiled. The problem was, to the religious men, these sorts of rituals had become just as important as the law itself. Their man-made rules had become more meaningful than the commands God had given them.

The men were staring at Jesus expectantly, and he sighed. As he opened his mouth to speak, Jesus knew his words would cut right through to the heart of their religion. The battle was about to get ugly.

"You hypocrites! Isaiah was right when he prophesied about you, for he wrote,

> 'These people honour me with their lips,
>   but their hearts are far from me.
> Their worship is a farce,
>   for they teach man-made ideas as commands from God.'

For you ignore God's law and substitute your own tradition."

The Pharisees and the teachers of religious law were outraged, but Jesus went on. "You skilfully sidestep God's law in order to hold on to your own tradition. For instance, Moses gave you this law from God: 'Honour your father and mother,' and 'Anyone who speaks disrespectfully of father or mother must be put to death.' But you say it is all right for people to say to their parents, 'Sorry, I can't help you. For I have vowed to give to God what I would have given to you.' In this way, you let them disregard their needy parents. And so you cancel the word of God in order to hand down your own tradition. And this is only one example among many others."

Jesus turned and called out to the crowd. "Listen and try to understand. It's not what goes into your mouth that defiles you; you are defiled by the words that come out of your mouth."

Jesus walked away, leaving the religious leaders to fume over his words. His disciples asked him, "Do you realise you offended the Pharisees by what you just said?"

Jesus replied, "Every plant not planted by my heavenly Father will be uprooted, so ignore them. They are blind guides leading the blind, and if one blind person guides another, they will both fall into a ditch."

The disciples grinned at one another. Then their faces turned serious and they asked Jesus what he had meant when he said that people aren't defiled by what they eat. The law of Moses specified clean animals that could be eaten, such as sheep, fish, locusts and cows. And unclean animals that could not be eaten, such as camels, hares, pigs, marine mammals, eagles, vultures, pelicans, mice and lizards. The Jews could not even touch the dead body of an unclean animal or they would be defiled.

"Don't you understand either?" Jesus asked. "Can't you see that the food you put into your body cannot defile you? Food doesn't go into your heart, but only passes through the stomach and then goes into the sewer."

The disciples scratched their heads in amazement. Jesus was declaring that all food was clean. He was making a new covenant with mankind, and everything would be different. Jesus explained, "It is what comes from inside that defiles you. For from within, out of a person's heart, come evil thoughts, sexual immorality, theft, murder, adultery, greed, wickedness, deceit, lustful desires, envy, slander, pride, and foolishness. These are what defile you. Eating with unwashed hands will never defile you."

The disciples were beginning to realise that performing rituals and following rules to look good on the outside would no longer work. If God could examine a person's heart and see him from the inside out, righteousness would be impossible to fake.

69.

The Faith of a Gentile Woman

Matthew 15:21-28, Mark 7:24-30

The Pharisees and the teachers of religious law were furious with Jesus. Tension was mounting in Galilee and a major religious conflict could erupt at any moment. So Jesus quietly left the area. He travelled north to the Gentile cities of Tyre and Sidon. He tried not to let anyone know he was there, but as usual, the news of his arrival spread quickly. A Greek woman, who was born in Syrian Phoenicia, came to find him. She followed him and begged him, "Have mercy on me, O Lord, Son of David! For my daughter is possessed by a demon that torments her severely."

Jesus kept walking, but she followed and continued to plead with him until the disciples grew annoyed. "Tell her to go away," they said. "She is bothering us with all her begging."

Jesus turned and looked at the woman. His face was filled with compassion and he told her, "I was sent only to help God's lost sheep - the people of Israel."

They kept walking but the Gentile woman would not leave. Instead, she fell at Jesus' feet, and cried, "Lord, help me!"

Jesus looked down and considered the woman. Then he said with a slow smile, "It isn't right to take food from the children and throw it to the dogs."

The woman knew if she received just the smallest amount of his power it would be enough. She replied without missing a beat, "That's true, Lord, but even the dogs under the table are allowed to eat the scraps from the children's plates."

Jesus' eyes lit up and he laughed.

"Good answer!" he said. "Now go home, for the demon has left your daughter."

The woman ran all the way home and when she arrived she found her little girl lying quietly in bed. The demon was gone.

70.

Jesus Feeds Four Thousand

Matthew 15:29-39, Mark 7:31-37, 8:1-10

When Jesus returned to the Sea of Galilee, he went to the region of the Decapolis, the Ten Cities. Some people came to him with a man who was deaf and could hardly talk. They begged Jesus to lay his hands on the man and heal him. Jesus led him away from the crowd. He put his fingers into the man's ears, then he spat on his own fingers and touched the man's tongue. He looked up to heaven and with a great sigh, said, "Ephphatha!" which means, "Be opened!"

At once the man could hear perfectly and he began to speak! Jesus took him back to the crowd and told them not to tell anyone what had happened. But the more he told them not to spread the news, the faster the news spread. Everybody was completely amazed, and they could not stop talking about it. "Everything he does is wonderful. He even makes the deaf to hear and gives speech to those who cannot speak."

Jesus went up and sat on the mountainside, and it wasn't long before the crowds came. They brought the lame, the crippled, the blind, the mute and many others with them, and Jesus healed them all. Those who were lame and crippled began to walk, those who were blind could see, and those who were mute began to speak! The people in the crowd were full of joy as they praised the God of Israel.

In the afternoon on the third day, Jesus called his disciples together. He said, "I feel sorry for these people. They have been here with me for three days, and they have nothing left to eat. I don't want to send them away hungry, or they will faint along the way."

The disciples looked out over the crowd and frowned. "Where would we get enough food here in the wilderness for such a huge crowd?"

Jesus looked at them with a twinkle in his eye. "How much bread do you have?"

Their eyes lit up as they answered, "Seven loaves, and a few small fish."

Jesus told the people to sit down, then he looked to heaven and thanked God. The disciples watched him closely as he began to break the loaves and fish into pieces. He passed the food to them and they passed it out to the crowd. There were about four thousand men, and many more women and children. When they were all satisfied, the disciples collected seven large baskets of leftovers. Jesus sent the crowds on their way, then he got into the boat with his disciples and they crossed to the other side of the sea.

71.

The Pharisees Demand a Sign

Matthew 12:38-45, 16:1-4,
Mark 8:11-13, Luke 11:29-32

The boat landed on the shore at Magdala, and Jesus climbed out. He was immediately greeted by a group of Pharisees striding towards him. Their robes flapped behind them as they demanded, "Teacher, we want you to show us a miraculous sign to prove your authority."

Jesus looked into the Pharisee's stony faces. He knew even the most sensational miracle would never be enough for them. Their eyes were blind to the things they didn't want to see, and their ears were deaf to the things they didn't want to hear. They refused to recognise the greatest sign of all: God's very own Son.

Jesus sighed, "Only an evil, adulterous generation would demand a miraculous sign; but the only sign I will give them is the sign of the prophet Jonah. For as Jonah was in the belly of the great fish for three days and three nights, so will the Son of Man be in the heart of the earth for three days and three nights.

"The people of Nineveh will stand up against this generation on judgment day and condemn it, for they repented of their sins at the preaching of Jonah. Now someone greater than Jonah is here - but you refuse to repent. The queen of Sheba will also stand up against this generation on judgment day and condemn it, for she came from a distant land to hear the wisdom of Solomon. Now someone greater than Solomon is here - but you refuse to listen.

"You know the saying, 'Red sky at night means fair weather tomorrow; red sky in the morning means foul weather all day.' You know how to interpret the weather signs in the sky, but you don't know how to interpret the signs of the times!"

The Pharisees scowled in anger, but they had no reply. So Jesus and his disciples got into the boat and crossed the sea once more.

72.

The Yeast of the Pharisees and Sadducees

Matthew 16:5-12, Mark 8:14-21

One by one, the disciples realised they had forgotten to bring food on the boat with them. They were in the middle of the sea and the city of Magdala was a small dot on the horizon behind them. Jesus watched as their faces turned to frowns.

"Watch out!" he warned them. "Beware of the yeast of the Pharisees and Sadducees."

The men didn't know what he meant, and they began to argue and blame one another for not bringing the food. Jesus looked on in dismay, and asked them, "Why are you arguing about having no bread? Don't you know or understand even yet? Are your hearts too hard to take it in? 'You have eyes - can't you see? You have ears - can't you hear?' Don't you remember anything at all? When I fed the 5,000 with five loaves of bread, how many baskets of leftovers did you pick up afterward?"

The disciples answered sheepishly. "Twelve."

"And when I fed the 4,000 with seven loaves, how many large baskets of leftovers did you pick up?"

"Seven," they said.

"Don't you understand yet?" he asked them.

The men stared at Jesus, and realised he wasn't talking about the yeast that was used to make bread. The yeast he was talking about was the hypocrisy and false teaching of the Pharisees and Sadducees. So many of their human ideas had been mixed in with God's truth, that the truth itself was completely hidden from them.

73.

Peter's Declaration

Matthew 16:13-20,
Mark 8:27-30, Luke 9:18-20

Simon Peter bent down and flicked a stone from his sandal. They had been walking all day, heading north, towards the villages of Caesarea Philippi. Jesus had been silent for most of the journey, but he suddenly interrupted their conversation. "Who do people say I am?"

The disciples looked at him sideways as they continued walking. "Well," they replied, "some say John the Baptist, some say Elijah, and others say you are one of the other ancient prophets risen from the dead."

Jesus nodded and thought about it. Then he asked, "But who do you say I am?"

Peter stared straight at Jesus and answered without hesitating, "You are the Messiah, the Son of the living God."

Jesus grinned and put his arm around Peter's neck. "You are blessed, Simon son of John, because my Father in heaven has revealed this to you. You did not learn this from any human being. Now I say to you that you are Peter (which means 'rock'), and upon this rock I will build my church, and all the powers of hell will not conquer it."

Blood rushed to Peter's cheeks and he beamed at such a compliment. He knew he was nobody special, just a humble fisherman who often made decisions too quickly and spoke too soon. But he had Jesus' approval and that was all that mattered. He stood a little straighter and held his chest a little higher as they continued on their way. Jesus' words echoed in Peter's mind, but he had no idea they were prophetic of what was to come. This humble, bumbling fisherman would become one of the great foundational rocks of the early church.

74.

Jesus Predicts His Death

Matthew 16:21-28,
Mark 8:31-38, Luke 9:21-27

The disciples now knew that Jesus was the Messiah, and they had confessed their faith in him. But Jesus told them not to tell anybody. First, he had to reveal God's plan to them, so they could fully understand what he had come to do. Jesus told them he would go to Jerusalem and suffer many terrible things. He would be rejected by the elders, the leading priests and the teachers of religious law. He would be betrayed into the hands of his enemies and be killed. But then on the third day he would be raised to life.

As Jesus told them these things, the disciples looked at one another in alarm and did not understand what he meant. A dead Messiah made no sense at all.

Simon Peter pulled Jesus aside and privately reprimanded him. "Heaven forbid, Lord," he said. "This will never happen to you!"

Jesus knew Peter spoke out of love, but he would not be tempted away from his mission. "Get away from me, Satan!" he said to Peter in a low voice. "You are a dangerous trap to me. You are seeing things merely from a human point of view, not from God's."

Peter stepped back, wounded and confused. His shoulders sagged and his heart suddenly ached.

Jesus breathed out slowly, then called the crowd to join his disciples. He told them all plainly, "If any of you wants to be my follower, you must give up your own way, take up your cross, and follow me. If you try to hang on to your life, you will lose it. But if you give up your life for my sake and for the sake of the Good News, you will save it. And what do you benefit if you gain the whole world but lose your own soul? Is anything worth more than your soul? If anyone is ashamed of me and my message in these adulterous and sinful days, the Son of Man will be ashamed of that person when he returns in the glory of his Father with the holy angels."

75.

The Transfiguration

Matthew 17:1-13,
Mark 9:2-13, Luke 9:28-36

Six days later, Jesus took Simon Peter, James and John with him and they went up on a high mountain to pray. As Jesus began to pray, the three men suddenly gasped. They stared in awe as his face began to shine like the sun, and his clothes became as white as the light. Then Moses and Elijah appeared out of nowhere to stand with Jesus. They talked quietly with him about his departure from the world, which would be fulfilled in Jerusalem.

Peter's jaw dropped open and he shook his head in surprise. His wide eyes darted from Elijah to Moses and back again. He could not believe two of the most famous men in the history of Israel were standing right in front of him. Moses was the lawgiver and Elijah was the greatest prophet who had ever lived. Peter did not know what to say, and before he could stop himself, he blurted out, "Lord, it's wonderful for us to be here! If you want, I'll make three shelters as memorials - one for you, one for Moses, and one for Elijah."

Before Peter could finish speaking, a bright cloud came and overshadowed them. Peter and the other two disciples froze as a powerful voice came from the cloud. "This is my dearly loved Son, who brings me great joy. Listen to him."

The three disciples were terrified and fell face down on the ground. They cowered there with their eyes tightly closed until Jesus came over and gently touched them. "Get up. Don't be afraid."

When the men looked up, Moses and Elijah were gone, and they stared at Jesus in stunned amazement. As Jesus led the way back down the mountain, he said to them, "Don't tell anyone what you have seen until the Son of Man has been raised from the dead."

The disciples agreed to keep it to themselves, but they wondered what Jesus meant when he said, "raised from the dead."

When they were almost at the base of the mountain, they asked Jesus, "Why do the teachers of religious law insist that Elijah must return before the Messiah comes?"

Jesus replied, "Elijah is indeed coming first to get everything ready. But I tell you, Elijah has already come, but he wasn't recognised, and they chose to abuse him. And in the same way they will also make the Son of Man suffer."

Peter glanced at John, and they both frowned as they realised Jesus was talking about John the Baptist, who had come in the spirit and power of Elijah. For the rest of the descent the men were silent. They stole glances at Jesus and wondered what on earth was going on.

76.

Jesus Heals a Boy with a Demon

Matthew 17:14-20,
Mark 9:14-29, Luke 9:37-43a

The other disciples had been waiting for Jesus at the base of the mountain. As Jesus came down, he saw that a large crowd had circled around them. The teachers of religious law were in their faces, and a heated argument had broken out. When the crowd saw Jesus coming, they ran to meet him. He asked them, "What is all this arguing about?"

A man pushed to the front of the crowd and cried out, "Teacher, I brought my son so you could heal him. He is possessed by an evil spirit that won't let him talk. And whenever this spirit seizes him, it throws him violently to the ground. Then he foams at the mouth and grinds his teeth and becomes rigid. So I asked your disciples to cast out the evil spirit, but they couldn't do it."

The disciples looked at Jesus helplessly.

Jesus frowned and said, "You faithless people! How long must I be with you? How long must I put up with you? Bring the boy to me."

The crowd made way for the boy to come, but as soon as the evil spirit saw Jesus, it threw the boy into a violent convulsion. His small body fell to the ground, writhing and foaming at the mouth.

"How long has this been happening?" Jesus asked the boy's distressed father.

He replied, "Since he was a little boy. The spirit often throws him into the fire or into water, trying to kill him. Have mercy on us and help us, if you can."

"What do you mean, 'If I can'?" Jesus asked. "Anything is possible if a person believes."

"I do believe, but help me overcome my unbelief!" the man cried desperately.

The crowd around them was growing and people were running over to see what was happening. Jesus looked down at the boy and rebuked the evil spirit. "Listen, you spirit that makes this boy unable to hear and speak. I command you to come out of this child and never enter him again!"

The spirit screamed and threw the boy into one last violent convulsion as it left. The people in the crowd gasped and stared at the boy's limp body laying on the ground. They were sure he was dead, but to their amazement, Jesus bent down and helped him to his feet. Tears filled the man's eyes as he took his son in his arms and buried his face in his hair.

When they were alone again in the house, the disciples asked Jesus, "Why couldn't we cast out that evil spirit?"

Jesus told them, "This kind can be cast out only by prayer."

77.

Jesus Predicts His Death Again

Matthew 17:22-23,
Mark 9:30-32, Luke 9:43b-45

Jesus had reached the peak of his mission and he knew he would soon be on the final road to Jerusalem. He still had many things to teach his disciples, so they slipped away from the crowds and travelled through Galilee without anybody knowing.

When they were alone, Jesus gathered his men together. "Listen to me and remember what I say. The Son of Man is going to be betrayed into the hands of his enemies. He will be killed, but three days later he will rise from the dead."

Jesus' words were clear, but their meaning was still hidden from the disciples. They stared at him in dismay and their hearts were filled with sorrow, but they were too afraid to ask him what he meant.

78.

The Temple Tax

Matthew 17:24-27

Tax booths were popping up all over Judea and Galilee. It was the time of year when every Jewish male over the age of twenty-one had to pay a half-shekel for the Temple tax. Simon Peter was minding his own business when some tax collectors approached him with a sneer. "Doesn't your teacher pay the Temple tax?"

Peter frowned, "Yes, he does."

He went back to the house and walked in the door. Before he could say anything, Jesus asked him, "What do you think, Peter? Do kings tax their own people or the people they have conquered?"

"They tax the people they have conquered," Peter replied.

"Well, then," Jesus smiled, "the citizens are free! However, we don't want to offend them, so go down to the lake and throw in a line. Open the mouth of the first fish you catch, and you will find a large silver coin. Take it and pay the tax for both of us."

Peter went down to the sea and it wasn't long before a fish was flipping about on the end of his line. He carefully unhooked it and looked over his shoulder to see if anyone was watching. Then he slowly opened the mouth of the fish. When he saw the silver coin inside, he sat back and laughed out loud. It was a shekel, exactly the amount he needed. With a grin, he took the coin and slid the fish gently back into the water. Then he hurried away to pay the tax and tell the other disciples what had happened.

79.

The Greatest in the Kingdom

Matthew 18:1-5,
Mark 9:33-37, Luke 9:46-48

As they travelled back to Capernaum, Jesus walked on ahead. The disciples lagged behind, and as they walked, they began to argue about who was the greatest among them. Jesus waited until they had arrived at the house, then he asked them, "What were you discussing out on the road?"

The disciples looked at one another sheepishly and then down at the ground. Nobody would answer, but Jesus already knew what they had been talking about. He told them, "Whoever wants to be first must take last place and be the servant of everyone else."

A small boy was at the house and Jesus scooped him up in his arms. The disciples raised their eyes to meet his gaze. "I tell you the truth, unless you turn from your sins and become like little children, you will never get into the Kingdom of Heaven. So anyone who becomes as humble as this little child is the greatest in the Kingdom of Heaven. Anyone who welcomes a little child like this on my behalf welcomes me, and anyone who welcomes me also welcomes my Father who sent me. Whoever is the least among you is the greatest."

80.

Using the Name of Jesus

Matthew 18:6-10, Mark 9:38-48,
Luke 9:49-50, 17:1-2

John's face was flushed as he burst into the house to find Jesus. "Teacher, we saw someone using your name to cast out demons, but we told him to stop because he wasn't in our group."

John huffed with indignation, but Jesus told him, "Don't stop him! No one who performs a miracle in my name will soon be able to speak evil of me. Anyone who is not against us is for us. If anyone gives you even a cup of water because you belong to the Messiah, I tell you the truth, that person will surely be rewarded."

John squirmed at the gentle rebuke and felt suddenly deflated. The disciples had been with Jesus for over two years, but his words continued to astound them. So many of the things they thought were right, were wrong, and so many things they thought were wrong, turned out to be right! Jesus met each of his disciples' eyes. There was so much for them to learn about the Kingdom of God. To be a part of it was far more valuable than anything they could own or do here in this lifetime.

When Jesus spoke again his voice was full of tenderness. "But if you cause one of these little ones who trusts in me to fall into sin, it would be better for you to be thrown into the sea with a large millstone hung around your neck. If your hand causes you to sin, cut it off. It's better to enter eternal life with only one hand than to go into the unquenchable fires of hell with two hands. If your foot causes you to sin, cut it off. It's better to enter eternal life with only one foot than to be thrown into hell with two feet. And if your eye causes you to sin, gouge it out. It's better to enter the Kingdom of God with only one eye than to have two eyes and be thrown into hell, 'where the maggots never die and the fire never goes out.'"

81.

Parable of the Unforgiving Servant

Matthew 18:15-35, Luke 17:3-4

Jesus taught his disciples how to correct another believer. "If another believer sins against you, go privately and point out the offense. If the other person listens and confesses it, you have won that person back. But if you are unsuccessful, take one or two others with you and go back again, so that everything you say may be confirmed by two or three witnesses. If the person still refuses to listen, take your case to the church. Then if he or she won't accept the church's decision, treat that person as a pagan or a corrupt tax collector."

Peter asked Jesus, "Lord, how often should I forgive someone who sins against me? Seven times?"

"No, not seven times," Jesus replied, "but seventy times seven!"

Peter frowned. He thought he was being generous if he forgave somebody seven times. Jesus smiled and told him a parable. "The Kingdom of Heaven can be compared to a king who decided to bring his accounts up to date with servants who had borrowed money from him. In the process, one of his debtors was brought in who owed him millions of dollars. He couldn't pay, so his master ordered that he be sold - along with his wife, his children, and everything he owned - to pay the debt.

"But the man fell down before his master and begged him, 'Please, be patient with me, and I will pay it all.' Then his master was filled with pity for him, and he released him and forgave his debt.

"But when the man left the king, he went to a fellow servant who owed him a few thousand dollars. He grabbed him by the throat and demanded instant payment.

"His fellow servant fell down before him and begged for a little more time. 'Be patient with me, and I will pay it,' he pleaded. But his creditor wouldn't wait. He had the man arrested and put in prison until the debt could be paid in full.

"When some of the other servants saw this, they were very upset. They went to the king and told him everything that had happened. Then the king called in the man he had forgiven and said, 'You evil servant! I forgave you that tremendous debt because you pleaded with me. Shouldn't you have mercy on your fellow servant, just as I had mercy on you?' Then the angry king sent the man to prison to be tortured until he had paid his entire debt.

"That's what my heavenly Father will do to you if you refuse to forgive your brothers and sisters from your heart."

82.

Marriage and Divorce

Matthew 19:1-12, Mark 10:1-12, Luke 16:18

Jesus left Capernaum and went down to Judea, to an area east of the Jordan River. As usual, the crowds followed, and he taught them and healed many people. It wasn't long before the Pharisees showed up and surrounded him. They were desperate to discredit Jesus and turn the people against him, and they had thought of the perfect controversial question to trap him with.

"Should a man be allowed to divorce his wife for just any reason?" they asked.

As always, Jesus pointed them back to the truth. "Haven't you read the Scriptures? They record that from the beginning 'God made them male and female.'"

The crowd was silent as Jesus continued, "'This explains why a man leaves his father and mother and is joined to his wife, and the two are united into one.' Since they are no longer two but one, let no one split apart what God has joined together."

The Pharisees were smug because they had already prepared their answer. "Then why did Moses say in the law that a man could give his wife a written notice of divorce and send her away?"

Their gleaming eyes were locked on Jesus' face and they were eager to hear how he would answer this apparent contradiction of Scripture. But Jesus would never be drawn into their traps. He would always have an answer to silence the critics.

"Moses permitted divorce only as a concession to your hard hearts, but it was not what God had originally intended. And I tell you this, whoever divorces his wife and marries someone else commits adultery - unless his wife has been unfaithful. And if a woman divorces her husband and marries someone else, she commits adultery."

The Pharisees narrowed their eyes and skulked away to plan their next attack.

83.

Jesus Blesses the Children

Matthew 19:13-15,
Mark 10:13-16, Luke 18:15-17

iggles and high-pitched squeals filled the air. Many parents had brought their little children to Jesus, hoping he might lay his hands on them and bless them. But when the disciples saw them coming, they began to shoo them away. They scolded the parents and told them not to bother Jesus.

When Jesus saw what was happening, he rebuked his disciples. He called the children over, and they ran to him with huge smiles and wide eyes. Jesus sat with them and listened to them and laughed in delight at all the things they said. Then he put his hands on the children's heads, blessing them and praying for them.

His eyes shone as he told his disciples, "Let the children come to me. Don't stop them! For the Kingdom of God belongs to those who are like these children. I tell you the truth, anyone who doesn't receive the Kingdom of God like a child will never enter it."

84.

The Rich Young Man

Matthew 19:16-30,
Mark 10:17-31, Luke 18:18-30

Jesus was about to leave the area when a young man ran up and knelt at his feet.

"Good Teacher, what must I do to inherit eternal life?" he asked.

"Why do you call me good?" Jesus asked. "Only God is truly good. But to answer your question, you know the commandments: 'You must not murder. You must not commit adultery. You must not steal. You must not testify falsely. You must not cheat anyone. Honour your father and mother.'"

"Teacher," the man declared eagerly, "I've obeyed all these commandments since I was young."

Jesus smiled sadly at the man's answer and his heart overflowed with love for him. The man's problem was that he did not recognise he was a sinner.

"There is still one thing you haven't done," Jesus said, as he helped the man to his feet. "Go and sell all your possessions and give the money to the poor, and you will have treasure in heaven. Then come, follow me."

The young man's face fell because he was very rich and had many possessions. He stood there for a long moment, wrestling with the decision Jesus was asking him to make. Finally, he turned and walked away in disappointment. The young man failed the test by deciding his possessions and the things of this world were more important to him than following Jesus.

Jesus sadly watched him go. "How hard it is for the rich to enter the Kingdom of God! In fact, it is easier for a camel to go through the eye of a needle than for a rich person to enter the Kingdom of God!"

The disciples were astonished, and they asked, "Then who in the world can be saved?"

Jesus told them, "Humanly speaking, it is impossible. But not with God. Everything is possible with God."

Simon Peter stepped forward. "We've given up everything to follow you."

Jesus put his hand on Peter's shoulder. "Yes," he replied, "and I assure you that everyone who has given up house or brothers or sisters or mother or father or children or property, for my sake and for the Good News, will receive now in return a hundred times as many houses, brothers, sisters, mothers, children, and property - along with persecution. And in the world to come that person will have eternal life. But many who are the greatest now will be least important then, and those who seem least important now will be the greatest then."

85.
Parable of the Vineyard Workers

Matthew 20:1-16

"For the Kingdom of Heaven is like the landowner who went out early one morning to hire workers for his vineyard. He agreed to pay the normal daily wage and sent them out to work.

"At nine o'clock in the morning he was passing through the marketplace and saw some people standing around doing nothing. So he hired them, telling them he would pay them whatever was right at the end of the day. So they went to work in the vineyard. At noon and again at three o'clock he did the same thing.

"At five o'clock that afternoon he was in town again and saw some more people standing around. He asked them, 'Why haven't you been working today?'

"They replied, 'Because no one hired us.'

"The landowner told them, 'Then go out and join the others in my vineyard.'

"That evening he told the foreman to call the workers in and pay them, beginning with the last workers first. When those hired at five o'clock were paid, each received a full day's wage. When those hired first came to get their pay, they assumed they would receive more. But they, too, were paid a day's wage. When they received their pay, they protested to the owner, 'Those people worked only one hour, and yet you've paid them just as much as you paid us who worked all day in the scorching heat.'

"He answered one of them, 'Friend, I haven't been unfair! Didn't you agree to work all day for the usual wage? Take your money and go. I wanted to pay this last worker the same as you. Is it against the law for me to do what I want with my money? Should you be jealous because I am kind to others?'

"So those who are last now will be first then, and those who are first will be last."

86.

The Festival of Shelters

John 7:1-31

Jesus returned to Galilee and travelled around the region. He wanted to stay away from Judea, because he knew the Jewish leaders were plotting to kill him. But the Festival of Shelters was drawing near, and his brothers, James, Joseph, Simon and Judas, began to mock him and pressure him to go to Jerusalem for the festival. They thought Jesus was a phony, and they scoffed, "Leave here and go to Judea, where your followers can see your miracles! You can't become famous if you hide like this! If you can do such wonderful things, show yourself to the world!"

They roared with laughter and sneered at him, but Jesus ignored them. He told them, "Now is not the right time for me to go, but you can go anytime. The world can't hate you, but it does hate me because I accuse it of doing evil. You go on. I'm not going to this festival, because my time has not yet come."

His brothers shook their heads and set out for Jerusalem. When they were gone, Jesus followed in secret, but he was careful to stay out of sight.

Meanwhile in Jerusalem, the Jewish leaders were looking for Jesus and asking everyone if they had seen him. Nobody had, but everybody was talking about him.

Some argued, "He's a good man," but others said, "He's nothing but a fraud who deceives the people."

Nobody was brave enough to say good things about him in public though, because they were afraid of the Jewish leaders.

Halfway through the festival, Jesus came out of hiding and walked boldly through the streets, right up to the Temple. The people flocked to him as he began to preach, and they were completely amazed by the things he said.

"How does he know so much when he hasn't been trained?" they wondered.

Jesus knew what they were thinking and told them, "My message is not my own; it comes from God who sent me. Anyone who wants to do the will of God will know whether my teaching is from God or is merely my own. Those who speak for themselves want glory only for themselves, but a person who seeks to honour the one who sent him speaks truth, not lies. Moses gave you the law, but none of you obeys it! In fact, you are trying to kill me."

The people in the crowd were baffled. "You're demon possessed!" they cried. "Who's trying to kill you?"

Jesus replied, "I did one miracle on the Sabbath, and you were amazed. But you work on the Sabbath, too, when you obey Moses' law of circumcision. (Actually, this tradition of circumcision began with the patriarchs, long before the law of Moses.) For if the correct time for circumcising your son falls on the Sabbath, you go ahead and do it so as not to break the law of Moses. So why should you be angry with me for healing a man on the Sabbath? Look beneath the surface so you can judge correctly."

The Pharisees stood at the edge of the crowd, and they watched Jesus with daggers in their eyes. They had no reply for his clever arguments, and they were fuming. The people were confused as they looked at the Pharisees and then back at Jesus.

"Isn't this the man they are trying to kill?" they asked one another. "But here he is, speaking in public, and they say nothing to him. Could our leaders possibly believe that he is the Messiah? But how could he be? For we know where this man comes from. When the Messiah comes, he will simply appear; no one will know where he comes from."

Jesus answered, "Yes, you know me, and you know where I come from. But I'm not here on my own. The one who sent me is true, and you don't know him. But I know him because I come from him, and he sent me to you."

Jesus' words grated on the Pharisees ears. To tell them they didn't know God was a bitter insult. They wanted to arrest him, but none of them touched him because his time had not yet come. Many people in the crowded Temple believed in him that day.

"After all," they said, "would you expect the Messiah to do more miraculous signs than this man has done?"

87.

The People Are Divided

John 7:32-52

When the Pharisees and the leading priests heard that more and more people in the crowd were turning to Jesus, their patience ran out and they sent officers to arrest him.

Jesus told the crowd, "I will be with you only a little longer. Then I will return to the one who sent me. You will search for me but not find me. And you cannot go where I am going."

The people frowned.

"Where is he planning to go?" they asked. "Is he thinking of leaving the country and going to the Jews in other lands? Maybe he will even teach the

Greeks! What does he mean when he says, 'You will search for me but not find me,' and 'You cannot go where I am going'?"

Finally, on the last and greatest day of the festival, a huge crowd gathered at the Temple to hear Jesus speak. His words pierced the air and every person in the crowd fell silent and leaned in to listen. "Anyone who is thirsty may come to me! Anyone who believes in me may come and drink! For the Scriptures declare, 'Rivers of living water will flow from his heart.'"

Jesus was talking about the Holy Spirit, who would be given to every person who believed in him after he had entered into his glory. But the people in the crowd didn't understand. There was division among them and nobody could agree. Some said he was a prophet, and some said he was the Messiah. But many others still could not believe the Messiah could possibly come from Galilee. Some people wanted him arrested, but nobody laid a hand on him.

When the officers who had been sent to arrest Jesus, returned empty handed, the Pharisees and the leading priests demanded, "Why didn't you bring him in?"

The officers shrugged helplessly. "We have never heard anyone speak like this!"

The Pharisees roared in outrage. "Have you been led astray, too? Is there a single one of us rulers or Pharisees who believes in him? This foolish crowd follows him, but they are ignorant of the law. God's curse is on them!"

A rumble of agreement rolled around the room. The leaders were furious that this simple man from Galilee, who had no training in the law, would quote Scripture to them and have so much influence on the people. The men were arguing furiously, when a single voice rose up in Jesus' defense. "Is it legal to convict a man before he is given a hearing?"

It was the voice of Nicodemus, the Pharisee who was a secret follower of Jesus. The other Pharisees turned on him and jeered, "Are you from Galilee, too? Search the Scriptures and see for yourself - no prophet ever comes from Galilee!"

88.

A Woman Caught in Adultery

John 8:1-11

At dawn the next morning, Jesus went back to the Temple. The people gathered around and he sat down to teach them. While he was speaking, a group of angry Pharisees and teachers of religious law suddenly barged through the crowd and hurled a woman before him. They pointed accusing fingers and glared at her in disdain.

"Teacher," they spat at Jesus, "this woman was caught in the act of adultery. The law of Moses says to stone her. What do you say?"

The woman stared at the ground, ashamed and terrified. Her heart was beating too quickly in her chest and she had nowhere to hide. The Pharisees and the teachers of religious law stared at Jesus with triumphant sneers. Surely they had him trapped this time. The seventh commandment was clear: "You must not commit adultery." If Jesus let the woman go, he would be contradicting the law of God.

Jesus did not look at the woman or her accusers. Instead, he bent down and began writing in the dust with his finger. The crowd watched in fascinated silence, but the religious leaders kept demanding an answer.

When Jesus finally stood up, he studied their hostile faces. "All right, but let the one who has never sinned throw the first stone!"

Then he bent down again and continued writing in the dust.

The religious men looked at one another in disbelief. Once again, Jesus had left them speechless. It wasn't long before they began to leave, one by one, starting with the oldest. When they were all gone, the woman looked up at Jesus. He was the only one without sin, and the only one with the right to throw stones. But he wouldn't do it. He hadn't come to punish the people and take their lives. He came to take their place.

He looked the woman in the eyes. "Where are your accusers? Didn't even one of them condemn you?"

"No, Lord," she replied shakily.

"Neither do I. Go and sin no more."

89.
The People Argue with Jesus

John 8:12-59

Jesus stayed in the Temple and continued to teach the people. "I am the light of the world. If you follow me, you won't have to walk in darkness, because you will have the light that leads to life."

It wasn't long before the Pharisees in the crowd began to heckle him. "You are making those claims about yourself! Such testimony is not valid." they scowled.

Jesus answered them easily, "These claims are valid even though I make them about myself. For I know where I came from and where I am going, but you don't know this about me. You judge me by human standards, but I do not judge anyone. And if I did, my judgment would be correct in every respect because I am not alone. The Father who sent me is with me. Your own law says that if two people agree about something, their witness is accepted as fact. I am one witness, and my Father who sent me is the other."

"Where is your father?" they challenged him.

"Since you don't know who I am, you don't know who my Father is. If you knew me, you would also know my Father."

The Jewish leaders shook their heads and murmured.

Later, Jesus told them, "I am going away. You will search for me but will die in your sin. You cannot come where I am going."

Nobody understand what he meant, and they asked themselves, "Is he planning to commit suicide? What does he mean, 'You cannot come where I am going'?"

Jesus continued, "You are from below; I am from above. You belong to this world; I do not. That is why I said that you will die in your sins; for unless you believe that I am who I claim to be, you will die in your sins."

"Who are you?" they demanded.

Jesus replied, "The one I have always claimed to be. I have much to say about you and much to condemn, but I won't. For I say only what I have heard from the one who sent me, and he is completely truthful. When you have lifted up the Son of Man on the cross, then you will understand that I am he. I do nothing on my own but say only what the Father taught me. And the one who sent me is with me - he has not deserted me. For I always do what pleases him."

There were many people in the crowd who believed in him as they listened to his words. Jesus told them, "You are truly my disciples if you remain faithful to my teachings. And you will know the truth, and the truth will set you free."

But the Pharisees and many other people in the crowd could not understand. They were too busy taking offense at everything he said, and they objected, "But we are descendants of Abraham. We have never been slaves to anyone. What do you mean, 'You will be set free'?"

Jesus replied, "I tell you the truth, everyone who sins is a slave of sin. A slave is not a permanent member of the family, but a son is part of the family forever. So if the Son sets you free, you are truly free. Yes, I realise that you are descendants of Abraham. And yet some of you are trying to kill me because there's no room in your hearts for my message. I am telling you what I saw when I was with my Father. But you are following the advice of your father."

"Our father is Abraham!" they insisted.

"No," Jesus replied, "for if you were really the children of Abraham, you would follow his example. Instead, you are trying to kill me because I told you the truth, which I heard from God. Abraham never did such a thing. No, you are imitating your real father."

The people were shocked and insulted. "We aren't illegitimate children!" they protested. "God himself is our true Father."

But Jesus told them, "If God were your Father, you would love me, because I have come to you from God. I am not here on my own, but he sent me. Why can't you understand what I am saying? It's because you can't even hear me!"

Jesus paused, before delivering the final devastating blow. "For you are the children of your father the devil, and you love to do the evil things he does. He was a murderer from the beginning. He has always hated the truth, because there is no truth in him. When he lies, it is consistent with his character; for he is a liar and the father of lies. So when I tell the truth, you just naturally don't believe me! Which of you can truthfully accuse me of sin? And since I am telling you the truth, why don't you believe me? Anyone who belongs to God listens gladly to the words of God. But you don't listen because you don't belong to God."

The people rose up against Jesus in furious defense. They were descendants of Abraham after all. Israel was God's chosen nation, and that made them the chosen ones. Jesus looked grimly across the angry crowd. The fact was, they broke their covenant partnership with God long ago. They were self-righteous, unrepentant and now they were livid. "You Samaritan devil! Didn't we say all along that you were possessed by a demon?"

"No," Jesus said, shaking his head sadly. "I have no demon in me. For I honour my Father - and you dishonour me. And though I have no wish to glorify myself, God is going to glorify me. He is the true judge. I tell you the truth, anyone who obeys my teaching will never die!"

The people sneered, "Now we know you are possessed by a demon. Even Abraham and the prophets died, but you say, 'Anyone who obeys my teaching will never die!' Are you greater than our father Abraham? He died, and so did the prophets. Who do you think you are?"

Jesus answered, "If I want glory for myself, it doesn't count. But it is my Father who will glorify me. You say, 'He is our God,' but you don't even know him. I know him. If I said otherwise, I would be as great a liar as you! But I do know him and obey him. Your father Abraham rejoiced as he looked forward to my coming. He saw it and was glad."

The people scoffed, "You aren't even fifty years old. How can you say you have seen Abraham?"

"I tell you the truth, before Abraham was even born, I am!"

The Pharisees had had enough. They were shaking with rage as they picked up stones to kill Jesus. But Jesus was hidden from them and he left the Temple unnoticed.

90.

Jesus Heals a Man Born Blind

Mark 8:22-26, John 9:1-34

One day Jesus and his disciples saw a blind beggar sitting by the side of the road. The man had been blind since he was born.

"Rabbi," the disciples asked as they came closer, "why was this man born blind? Was it because of his own sins or his parents' sins?"

Jesus stopped in front of the man and studied him with eyes full of compassion. It was a common belief among the Jews that disabilities and afflictions were caused by sin. They believed that God's hand of punishment was on people like this blind man. But the truth is, people who are suffering are especially loved by God, not cursed by Him.

Jesus told his disciples, "It was not because of his sins or his parents' sins. This happened so the power of God could be seen in him."

Jesus bent down and spat on the ground. He made mud with his saliva and then pressed the mud over the man's eyes. Then he told him to go and wash in the pool of Siloam. The disciples watched as the man shuffled away.

It was not long before the man came back. Only this time he wasn't shuffling, he was running! He ran straight to Jesus and looked him deep in the eyes. He could see! For the first time in his life, he could see. Jesus laughed and put his arm around the man's shoulders.

When his neighbours and other people who knew him realised he could see, they were astonished. They asked one another, "Isn't this the man who used to sit and beg?"

Some said yes, but others were not convinced. "No, he just looks like him!"

The man insisted, "Yes, I am the same one!"

The people were amazed, and they asked, "Who healed you? What happened?"

He told them, "The man they call Jesus made mud and spread it over my eyes and told me, 'Go to the pool of Siloam and wash yourself.' So I went and washed, and now I can see!"

"Where is he now?" they asked him.

But he did not know.

It just so happened to be the Sabbath, and some Pharisees came to investigate what was going on. They frowned when they saw the man who had been blind and asked him what happened.

The man repeated his story. "He put the mud over my eyes, and when I washed it away, I could see!"

Some of the Pharisees scowled and said, "This man Jesus is not from God, for he is working on the Sabbath."

Others were confused. "But how could an ordinary sinner do such miraculous signs?"

Nobody could agree. The Pharisees took the man aside to question him. "What's your opinion about this man who healed you?"

The man thought for a moment and replied, "I think he must be a prophet."

The Jewish leaders argued among themselves. Then they called for the man's parents because they did not believe the man had actually been blind.

"Is this your son? Was he born blind? If so, how can he now see?"

The man's parents looked at each other and replied nervously, "We know this is our son and that he was born blind, but we don't know how he can see or who healed him. Ask him. He is old enough to speak for himself."

They were afraid to say anything about Jesus, because the Jewish leaders had threatened that anyone who acknowledged Jesus as the Messiah, would be banned from the synagogue.

The leaders called the man back and spoke kindly to him. "God should get the glory for this, because we know this man Jesus is a sinner."

The man shrugged and laughed. "I don't know whether he is a sinner. But I know this: I was blind, and now I can see!"

"But what did he do?" the Pharisees asked in exasperation. "How did he heal you?"

"Look!" the man exclaimed. "I told you once. Didn't you listen? Why do you want to hear it again? Do you want to become his disciples, too?"

The Jewish leaders glared at the man and attacked him with insults. "You are his disciple, but we are disciples of Moses! We know God spoke to Moses, but we don't even know where this man comes from."

The man who had been blind laughed again. "Why, that's very strange! He healed my eyes, and yet you don't know where he comes from? We know that God doesn't listen to sinners, but he is ready to hear those who worship him and do his will. Ever since the world began, no one has been able to open the eyes of someone born blind. If this man were not from God, he couldn't have done it."

The leaders stood in silence with their mouths hanging open. They had no answer to the man's argument. They had already made up their minds about Jesus and would not listen to anybody who didn't share their opinion. In fact, they were outraged that the man was throwing their own teaching back at them, and they turned on him. "You were born a total sinner! Are you trying to teach us?"

Then they threw him out of the synagogue.

91.

Spiritual Blindness

John 9:35-41

When Jesus heard that the man had been thrown out of the synagogue, he went to find him. Jesus asked him, "Do you believe in the Son of Man?"

The man nodded eagerly. "Who is he, sir? I want to believe in him."

"You have seen him," Jesus said, "and he is speaking to you!"

"Yes, Lord, I believe!" the man said in awe. And he began to worship Jesus.

Then Jesus told him, "I entered this world to render judgment - to give sight to the blind and to show those who think they see that they are blind."

Some Pharisees who were standing nearby overheard Jesus and they were indignant. "Are you saying we're blind?"

"If you were blind, you wouldn't be guilty," Jesus replied. "But you remain guilty because you claim you can see.

92.

The Good Shepherd

John 10:1-21

The Pharisees were livid. Jesus turned and told the crowd, "I tell you the truth, anyone who sneaks over the wall of a sheepfold, rather than going through the gate, must surely be a thief and a robber! But the one who enters through the gate is the shepherd of the sheep. The gatekeeper opens the gate for him, and the sheep recognise his voice and come to him. He calls his own sheep by name and leads them out. After he has gathered his own flock, he walks ahead of them, and they follow him because they know his voice. They won't follow a stranger; they will run from him because they don't know his voice."

The people who heard Jesus' illustration didn't understand what he meant, so he explained it to them. "I tell you the truth, I am the gate for the sheep. All who came before me were thieves and robbers. But the true sheep did not listen to them. Yes, I am the gate. Those who come in through me will be saved. They will come and go freely and will find good pastures. The thief's purpose is to steal and kill and destroy. My purpose is to give them a rich and satisfying life.

"I am the good shepherd. The good shepherd sacrifices his life for the sheep. A hired hand will run when he sees a wolf coming. He will abandon the sheep because they don't belong to him and he isn't their shepherd. And so the wolf attacks them and scatters the flock. The hired hand runs away because he's working only for the money and doesn't really care about the sheep.

"I am the good shepherd; I know my own sheep, and they know me, just as my Father knows me and I know the Father. So I sacrifice my life for the sheep. I have other sheep, too, that are not in this sheepfold. I must bring them also. They will listen to my voice, and there will be one flock with one shepherd.

"The Father loves me because I sacrifice my life so I may take it back again. No one can take my life from me. I sacrifice it voluntarily. For I have the authority to lay it down when I want to and also to take it up again. For this is what my Father has commanded."

The people in the crowd began to argue, because they were still divided in their opinion of Jesus. Some people said, "He's demon possessed and out of his mind. Why listen to a man like that?"

But others were in awe and said, "This doesn't sound like a man possessed by a demon! Can a demon open the eyes of the blind?"

93.

Jesus Claims to be the Son of God Again

John 10:22-42

When winter came, Jesus returned to Jerusalem for Hanukkah, the Festival of Dedication. He went to the Temple, and while he was walking along the section known as Solomon's Colonnade, a group of Jews surrounded him.

They asked, "How long are you going to keep us in suspense? If you are the Messiah, tell us plainly."

Jesus answered, "I have already told you, and you don't believe me. The proof is the work I do in my Father's name. But you don't believe me because you are not my sheep. My sheep listen to my voice; I know them, and they follow me. I give them eternal life, and they will never perish. No one can snatch them away from me, for my Father has given them to me, and he is more powerful than anyone else. No one can snatch them from the Father's hand. The Father and I are one."

The Jews were furious at Jesus' answer and they picked up stones to kill him.

Jesus asked them calmly, "At my Father's direction I have done many good works. For which one are you going to stone me?"

"We're stoning you not for any good work, but for blasphemy!" they replied angrily. "You, a mere man, claim to be God."

Jesus sighed. "It is written in your own Scriptures that God said to certain leaders of the people, 'I say, you are gods!' And you know that the Scriptures cannot be altered. So if those people who received God's message were called 'gods,' why do you call it blasphemy when I say, 'I am the Son of God'? After all, the Father set me apart and sent me into the world. Don't believe me unless I carry out my Father's work. But if I do his work, believe in the evidence of the miraculous works I have done, even if you don't believe me. Then you will know and understand that the Father is in me, and I am in the Father."

The angry Jews tried to arrest Jesus, but he escaped them and left Jerusalem. He crossed the Jordan River and stayed at the place where John the Baptist had been preaching and baptising in the early days. Many people came to find him, and they believed in him.

"John didn't perform miraculous signs," they said to one another, "but everything he said about this man has come true."

94.

Parable of the Good Samaritan

Luke 10:25-37, Matthew 22:34-40

"Teacher, what should I do to inherit eternal life?"

Jesus studied the lawyer who had asked the question, then he asked one back. "What does the law of Moses say? How do you read it?"

The lawyer was an expert in the law, and he quoted it easily, "'You must love the Lord your God with all your heart, all your soul, all your strength, and all your mind.' And, 'Love your neighbour as yourself.'"

Jesus smiled. "Right! Do this and you will live!"

But the man frowned. Jesus hadn't told him anything new. He wanted to justify himself, so he asked another question. "And who is my neighbour?"

Jesus answered with the parable of the good Samaritan. "A Jewish man was travelling from Jerusalem down to Jericho, and he was attacked by bandits. They stripped him of his clothes, beat him up, and left him half dead beside the road.

"By chance a priest came along. But when he saw the man lying there, he crossed to the other side of the road and passed him by. A Temple assistant walked over and looked at him lying there, but he also passed by on the other side.

"Then a despised Samaritan came along, and when he saw the man, he felt compassion for him. Going over to him, the Samaritan soothed his wounds with olive oil and wine and bandaged them. Then he put the man on his own donkey and took him to an inn, where he took care of him. The next day he handed the innkeeper two silver coins, telling him, 'Take care of this man. If his bill runs higher than this, I'll pay you the next time I'm here.'

"Now which of these three would you say was a neighbour to the man who was attacked by bandits?" Jesus asked.

The lawyer replied, "The one who showed him mercy."

Jesus nodded, "Yes, now go and do the same."

95.

Mary and Martha

Luke 10:38-42

In the small town of Bethany, close to Jerusalem, a woman named Martha stood back to admire her work. She had been busy all day preparing a feast and everything was just right. Before she could rearrange the table settings one last time, she heard her guests arrive. She was thrilled to have Jesus in her home, and proudly welcomed him in. Then she raced back to the kitchen to check on the food.

Martha's sister, Mary, was also delighted that the guests had arrived. It wasn't proper for a woman to join the men's conversation, but Mary could not stay away. She dropped what she was doing and knelt at Jesus' feet, captivated by his words.

Meanwhile, Martha was rushing about, making sure the last tiny detail of the feast was perfect. When she noticed Mary, sitting motionless among the men, she could not believe her eyes!

She strode into the room and glared at Mary. Everybody was looking at her as she complained to Jesus, "Lord, doesn't it seem unfair to you that my sister just sits here while I do all the work? Tell her to come and help me."

Jesus smiled. "My dear Martha, you are worried and upset over all these details! There is only one thing worth being concerned about. Mary has discovered it, and it will not be taken away from her."

Mary's eyes shone as she followed her sister back to the kitchen to help serve a meal that would quickly be forgotten.

96.

A Warning Against Hypocrisy

Matthew 23:1-36, Luke 11:37-54

One day, a Pharisee invited Jesus to come and share a meal with him. As Jesus reclined at the man's table, the other guests watched him closely. When they realised he was not going to take part in the hand washing ceremony, they looked at one another in disgust.

Jesus sighed and met their accusing eyes. "You Pharisees are so careful to clean the outside of the cup and the dish, but inside you are filthy - full of greed and wickedness! Fools! Didn't God make the inside as well as the outside? First wash the inside of the cup and the dish, and then the outside will become clean, too."

The men murmured in indignation, but Jesus was just getting started. "What sorrow awaits you Pharisees. Hypocrites! For you are careful to tithe even the tiniest income from your herb gardens, but you ignore the more important aspects of the law - justice, mercy, and faith. You should tithe, yes, but do not neglect the more important things. Blind guides! You strain your water so you won't accidentally swallow a gnat, but you swallow a camel!

"What sorrow awaits you Pharisees. Hypocrites! For you are like whitewashed tombs - beautiful on the outside but filled on the inside with dead people's bones and all sorts of impurity. Outwardly you look like righteous people, but inwardly your hearts are filled with hypocrisy and lawlessness."

The Pharisees were outraged. How dare this rebel insult them! Their fists were clenched with fury and their eyes burned with resentment. They were ready to pounce on Jesus, but one of the experts of religious law held out his hand to calm them.

He spoke slowly, "Teacher, you have insulted us, too, in what you just said."

Jesus replied, "Yes, what sorrow also awaits you experts of religious law! For you crush people with unbearable religious demands, and you never lift a finger to ease the burden. What sorrow awaits you! For you build tombs for the prophets your ancestors killed, and you decorate the monuments of the godly people your ancestors destroyed. Then you say, 'If we had lived in the days of our ancestors, we would never have joined them in killing the prophets.'

"But in saying that, you testify against yourselves that you are indeed the descendants of those who murdered the prophets. Go ahead and finish what your ancestors started. Snakes! Sons of vipers! How will you escape the judgment of hell?

"Therefore, I am sending you prophets and wise men and teachers of religious law. But you will kill some by crucifixion, and you will flog others with whips in your synagogues, chasing them from city to city. As a result, you will be held responsible for the murder of all godly people of all time - from the murder of righteous Abel to the murder of Zechariah son of Berekiah, whom you killed in the Temple between the sanctuary and the altar. I tell you the truth, this judgment will fall on this very generation."

The man's jaw dropped, and his face burned with rage. They all began to attack Jesus with vicious questions, trying to make him say something they could use against him.

But Jesus continued, undaunted, "What sorrow awaits you teachers of religious law and you Pharisees. Hypocrites! For you shut the door of the Kingdom of Heaven in people's faces. You won't go in yourselves, and you don't let others enter either.

"What sorrow awaits you teachers of religious law and you Pharisees. Hypocrites! For you cross land and sea to make one convert, and then you turn that person into twice the child of hell you yourselves are!"

The men were irate, and they yelled savage insults at Jesus as he left the house.

Later, Jesus spoke to the crowds about them. "The teachers of religious law and the Pharisees are the official interpreters of the law of Moses. So practice and obey whatever they tell you, but don't follow their example. For they don't practice what they teach. Everything they do is for show. On their arms they wear extra wide prayer boxes with Scripture verses inside, and they wear robes with extra long tassels. And they love to sit at the head table at banquets and in the seats of honour in the synagogues. They love to receive respectful greetings as they walk in the marketplaces, and to be called 'Rabbi.' Don't let anyone call you 'Rabbi,' for you have only one teacher, and all of you are equal as brothers and sisters. And don't address anyone here on earth as 'Father,' for only God in heaven is your Father. And don't let anyone call you 'Teacher,' for you have only one teacher, the Messiah. The greatest among you must be a servant. But those who exalt themselves will be humbled, and those who humble themselves will be exalted."

97.

The Narrow Door

Luke 13:23-30

Jesus travelled through cities and villages, teaching the people as he went. One day somebody from the crowd called out, "Lord, will only a few be saved?"

Jesus answered, "Work hard to enter the narrow door to God's Kingdom, for many will try to enter but will fail. When the master of the house has locked the door, it will be too late. You will stand outside knocking and pleading, 'Lord, open the door for us!' But he will reply, 'I don't know you or where you come from.' Then you will say, 'But we ate and drank with you, and you taught in our streets.' And he will reply, 'I tell you, I don't know you or where you come from. Get away from me, all you who do evil.'

"There will be weeping and gnashing of teeth, for you will see Abraham, Isaac, Jacob, and all the prophets in the Kingdom of God, but you will be thrown out. And people will come from all over the world - from east and west, north and south - to take their places in the Kingdom of God. And note this: Some who seem least important now will be the greatest then, and some who are the greatest now will be least important then."

98.

Jesus Grieves for Jerusalem

Matthew 23:37-39, Luke 13:31-35

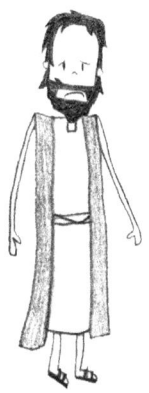

Not all of the Pharisees were against Jesus, and at that moment a group of them came to him with an urgent message. "Get away from here if you want to live! Herod Antipas wants to kill you!"

But Jesus replied, "Go tell that fox that I will keep on casting out demons and healing people today and tomorrow; and the third day I will accomplish my purpose. Yes, today, tomorrow, and the next day I must proceed on my way. For it wouldn't do for a prophet of God to be killed except in Jerusalem!"

Jesus turned away sadly. It was a tragic fact that most of the prophets sent from God had not been killed by foreign enemies, but by their own people. The people of Israel.

"O Jerusalem, Jerusalem, the city that kills the prophets and stones God's messengers! How often I have wanted to gather your children together as a hen protects her chicks beneath her wings, but you wouldn't let me. And now, look, your house is abandoned. And you will never see me again until you say, 'Blessings on the one who comes in the name of the Lord!'"

99.

A Rebellious Nation

Isaiah 1:10-20

About 700 years earlier, the prophet Isaiah had warned the people of Judah that their empty religion was detestable to God. They took part in the Temple rituals and looked like they were worshipping God from the outside, but their hearts were far from him. The people were full of hypocrisy, but though they dishonoured him with their secret sin and rebellion, God offered them hope and a way back to him.

Like all of the Old Testament prophets, Isaiah pointed the people to the coming King, the Saviour of the World. He would redeem even the most wretched sinners and take their place. It was as simple, yet as difficult, as giving up their sin and turning to him.

> Listen to the Lord, you leaders of "Sodom."
> Listen to the law of our God, people of "Gomorrah."
> "What makes you think I want all your sacrifices?"
> says the Lord.
> "I am sick of your burnt offerings of rams
> and the fat of fattened cattle.
> I get no pleasure from the blood
> of bulls and lambs and goats.
> When you come to worship me,

who asked you to parade through my courts with all your ceremony?
Stop bringing me your meaningless gifts;
    the incense of your offerings disgusts me!
As for your celebrations of the new moon and the Sabbath
    and your special days for fasting -
they are all sinful and false.
    I want no more of your pious meetings.
I hate your new moon celebrations and your annual festivals.
    They are a burden to me. I cannot stand them!
When you lift up your hands in prayer, I will not look.
    Though you offer many prayers, I will not listen,
    for your hands are covered with the blood of innocent victims.
Wash yourselves and be clean!
    Get your sins out of my sight.
    Give up your evil ways.
Learn to do good.
    Seek justice.
Help the oppressed.
    Defend the cause of orphans.
    Fight for the rights of widows.
"Come now, let's settle this,"
    says the Lord.
"Though your sins are like scarlet,
    I will make them as white as snow.
Though they are red like crimson,
    I will make them as white as wool.
If you will only obey me,
    you will have plenty to eat.
But if you turn away and refuse to listen,
    you will be devoured by the sword of your enemies.
    I, the Lord, have spoken!"

100.

Parable of the Rich Fool

Luke 12:13-34

The crowd around Jesus grew larger and larger, until thousands of people were trampling one another just to hear him speak. Somebody in the crowd yelled out, "Teacher, please tell my brother to divide our father's estate with me."

Jesus laughed and replied, "Friend, who made me a judge over you to decide such things as that?"

Then he addressed the whole crowd. "Beware! Guard against every kind of greed. Life is not measured by how much you own. A rich man had a fertile farm that produced fine crops. He said to himself, 'What should I do? I don't have room for all my crops.' Then he said, 'I know! I'll tear down my barns and build bigger ones. Then I'll have room enough to store all my wheat and other goods. And I'll sit back and say to myself, "My friend, you have enough stored away for years to come. Now take it easy! Eat, drink, and be merry!"'

"But God said to him, 'You fool! You will die this very night. Then who will get everything you worked for?'

"Yes, a person is a fool to store up earthly wealth but not have a rich relationship with God."

Jesus turned to his disciples and told them, "That is why I tell you not to worry about everyday life - whether you have enough food to eat or enough clothes to wear. For life is more than food, and your body more than clothing. Look at the ravens. They don't plant or harvest or store food in barns, for God feeds them. And you are far more valuable to him than any birds! Can all your worries add a single moment to your life? And if worry can't accomplish a little thing like that, what's the use of worrying over bigger things?

"Look at the lilies and how they grow. They don't work or make their clothing, yet Solomon in all his glory was not dressed as beautifully as they are. And if God cares so wonderfully for flowers that are here today and thrown into the fire tomorrow, he will certainly care for you. Why do you have so little faith?

"And don't be concerned about what to eat and what to drink. Don't worry about such things. These things dominate the thoughts of unbelievers all over the world, but your Father already knows your needs. Seek the Kingdom of God above all else, and he will give you everything you need.

"So don't be afraid, little flock. For it gives your Father great happiness to give you the Kingdom.

"Sell your possessions and give to those in need. This will store up treasure for you in heaven! And the purses of heaven never get old or develop holes. Your treasure will be safe; no thief can steal it and no moth can destroy it. Wherever your treasure is, there the desires of your heart will also be."

101.

A Call to Repentance

Luke 13:1-9

News travelled fast throughout Galilee, especially bad news. Pontius Pilate had heartlessly murdered a group of people from Galilee as they offered their sacrifices in the Temple. The disciples listened to the details in dismay and wondered what those people had done to deserve such a terrible death.

But Jesus shook his head. "Do you think those Galileans were worse sinners than all the other people from Galilee? Is that why they suffered? Not at all! And you will perish, too, unless you repent of your sins and turn to God. And what about the eighteen people who died when the tower in Siloam fell on them? Were they the worst sinners in Jerusalem? No, and I tell you again that unless you repent, you will perish, too."

Jesus paused, then he told them a parable that illustrated God's amazing patience and grace. "A man planted a fig tree in his garden and came again and again to see if there was any fruit on it, but he was always disappointed. Finally, he said to his gardener, 'I've waited three years, and there hasn't been a single fig! Cut it down. It's just taking up space in the garden.'

"The gardener answered, 'Sir, give it one more chance. Leave it another year, and I'll give it special attention and plenty of fertiliser. If we get figs next year, fine. If not, then you can cut it down.'"

102.

Jesus Heals on the Sabbath

Luke 13:10-17

There was a woman in the synagogue who had been crippled by an evil spirit. Her body was bent over and she had not been able to stand upright for eighteen years. Jesus noticed her and called her over. "Dear woman, you are healed of your sickness!"

As he put his hand on her, she tentatively raised her head. Tears began to run down her face as her back straightened out and she found herself looking right into the eyes of Jesus. Through her tears, the woman began to praise God for his incredible grace and mercy.

The leader of the synagogue had been watching and he sighed in exasperation. "There are six days of the week for working," he announced loudly. "Come on those days to be healed, not on the Sabbath."

Jesus' smile disappeared and he turned on the religious leaders. "You hypocrites! Each of you works on the Sabbath day! Don't you untie your ox or your donkey from its stall on the Sabbath and lead it out for water? This dear woman, a daughter of Abraham, has been held in bondage by Satan for eighteen years. Isn't it right that she be released, even on the Sabbath?"

Jesus' enemies scowled in humiliation. But the rest of the people crowded around the woman, rejoicing at the amazing thing Jesus had done for her.

103.

Humility

Luke 14:1-14

On another Sabbath, Jesus was invited to the home of a prominent Pharisee. As he came up to the house, they all watched him closely because there was a man there who was suffering from dropsy. Jesus studied the man whose hands and legs were painfully swollen. He turned and asked the Pharisees, "Is it permitted in the law to heal people on the Sabbath day, or not?"

The Pharisees were silent, so Jesus took hold of the man and healed him. As he sent him on his way, Jesus turned to the Pharisees again and asked, "Which of you doesn't work on the Sabbath? If your son or your cow falls into a pit, don't you rush to get him out?"

The men still had no reply.

When it was time to eat, Jesus watched as the guests jostled for the seats of honour close to the head of the table. He told them, "When you are invited to a wedding feast, don't sit in the seat of honour. What if someone who is more distinguished than you has also been invited? The host will come and say, 'Give this person your seat.' Then you will be embarrassed, and you will have to take whatever seat is left at the foot of the table!

"Instead, take the lowest place at the foot of the table. Then when your host sees you, he will come and say, 'Friend, we have a better place for you!' Then you will be honoured in front of all the other guests. For those who exalt themselves will be humbled, and those who humble themselves will be exalted."

Then Jesus turned to the man who had invited him. "When you put on a luncheon or a banquet," he said, "don't invite your friends, brothers, relatives, and rich neighbours. For they will invite you back, and that will be your only reward. Instead, invite the poor, the crippled, the lame, and the blind. Then at the resurrection of the righteous, God will reward you for inviting those who could not repay you."

104.

A Samaritan Village Rejects Jesus

Luke 9:51-56

The disciples had been walking all day and were looking forward to resting at the next Samaritan village. Jesus had already sent messengers on ahead so they could prepare for his arrival. But as they came close to the village, the Samaritan people came out and refused to welcome Jesus into their homes.

James and John looked at each other and scowled. How dare those Samaritan dogs refuse the Lord! The brothers burned with pride and glared at the Samaritans in contempt. They said loudly, "Lord, should we call down fire from heaven to burn them up?"

Jesus turned on the two brothers and rebuked them sharply. "You don't realise what your hearts are like. For the Son of Man has not come to destroy people's lives, but to save them."

Jesus turned and walked in the direction of the next village. James and John trudged along behind. They did not realise that if Jesus had come to call down judgment on the world, those Samaritans would not be the only ones to burn. There would be no hope for anybody.

105.

The Cost of Following Jesus

Matthew 8:18-22, Luke 9:57-62, 14:25-33

Jesus stared straight ahead, deep in thought as he walked. His mind was on Jerusalem, and the cross that waited for him there. A huge crowd swarmed around him, and they chattered excitedly, oblivious to the tension in his heart. They were full of anticipation, sure that Jesus would soon be sitting on the throne, ruling with mighty power and defeating their enemies once and for all.

One of the teachers of religious law called out from the crowd, "Teacher, I will follow you wherever you go."

Jesus kept walking as he replied, "Foxes have dens to live in, and birds have nests, but the Son of Man has no place even to lay his head."

Somebody else who wanted to follow Jesus called out, "Lord, first let me return home and bury my father."

But Jesus told him, "Follow me now. Let the spiritually dead bury their own dead."

Another man called out, "Yes, Lord, I will follow you, but first let me say good-bye to my family."

Jesus stopped walking and turned around. His eyes burned into the crowd as they bumped to a halt. "Anyone who puts a hand to the plough and then looks back is not fit for the Kingdom of God."

Jesus turned and kept walking, and the eager crowd followed. He knew most of the people followed him because they loved his miracles, his glory and his power. But unless they understood that his mission on earth was a mission of sacrifice, their decision to follow him would not last and they would soon fall away. Jesus didn't come to gather huge crowds around him. He came to make true disciples, followers who truly understood his message and were willing to put aside their own lives to live for him.

He stopped walking again. He had to make sure the people had no illusions about what it meant to follow him. "If you want to be my disciple, you must, by comparison, hate everyone else - your father and mother, wife and children, brothers and sisters - yes, even your own life. Otherwise, you cannot be my disciple. And if you do not carry your own cross and follow me, you cannot be my disciple."

Jesus' eyes travelled over the earnest faces that stared back at him. "But don't begin until you count the cost. For who would begin construction of a building without first calculating the cost to see if there is enough money to finish it? Otherwise, you might complete only the foundation before running out of money, and then everyone would laugh at you. They would say, 'There's the person who started that building and couldn't afford to finish it!'

"Or what king would go to war against another king without first sitting down with his counselors to discuss whether his army of 10,000 could defeat the 20,000 soldiers marching against him? And if he can't, he will send a delegation to discuss terms of peace while the enemy is still far away. So you cannot become my disciple without giving up everything you own."

106.

Parable of the Lost Sheep and the Lost Coin

Matthew 18:12-14, Luke 15:1-10

Tax collectors, sinners and outcasts came from every direction to hear Jesus' message of grace and forgiveness. His gaze moved over the crowd, from one face to the next, and his heart was filled with love for every one of them.

But when the Pharisees saw the kinds of people who flocked to him, they muttered and complained to each other, "This man welcomes notorious sinners and even eats with them."

Jesus turned to them and told them a parable. "If a man has a hundred sheep and one of them gets lost, what will he do? Won't he leave the ninety-nine others in the wilderness and go to search for the one that is lost until he finds it? And when he has found it, he will joyfully carry it home on his shoulders. When he arrives, he will call together his friends and neighbours, saying, 'Rejoice with me because I have found my lost sheep.' In the same way, there is more joy in heaven over one lost sinner who repents and returns to God than over ninety-nine others who are righteous and haven't strayed away!"

The Pharisees grumbled as Jesus continued with another parable. "Or suppose a woman has ten silver coins and loses one. Won't she light a lamp and sweep the entire house and search carefully until she finds it? And when she finds it, she will call in her friends and neighbours and say, 'Rejoice with me because I have found my lost coin.' In the same way, there is joy in the presence of God's angels when even one sinner repents."

The Pharisees scowled. It was unfathomable to them that a holy and righteous God would seek out sinners like these men and women. Their sin and their lifestyles were despicable. The Pharisees gathered up their robes and turned away in disgust.

107.

Parable of the Lost Son

Luke 15:11-32

The crowd pressed in closer to Jesus. They were the outcasts, the losers, the hopeless sinners and the misfits. But Jesus loved them. No matter who they were or what they had done, nothing could make Jesus love them any more or any less. Nothing could separate them from the love of God.

Jesus had another parable for them. "A man had two sons. The younger son told his father, 'I want my share of your estate now before you die.' So his father agreed to divide his wealth between his sons.

"A few days later this younger son packed all his belongings and moved to a distant land, and there he wasted all his money in wild living. About the time his money ran out, a great famine swept over the land, and he began to starve. He persuaded a local farmer to hire him, and the man sent him into his fields to feed the pigs. The young man became so hungry that even the pods he was feeding the pigs looked good to him. But no one gave him anything.

"When he finally came to his senses, he said to himself, 'At home even the hired servants have food enough to spare, and here I am dying of hunger! I will go home to my father and say, "Father, I have sinned against both heaven and you, and I am no longer worthy of being called your son. Please take me on as a hired servant."'

"So he returned home to his father. And while he was still a long way off, his father saw him coming. Filled with love and compassion, he ran to his son, embraced him, and kissed him. His son said to him, 'Father, I have sinned against both heaven and you, and I am no longer worthy of being called your son.'

"But his father said to the servants, 'Quick! Bring the finest robe in the house and put it on him. Get a ring for his finger and sandals for his feet. And kill the calf we have been fattening. We must celebrate with a feast, for this son of mine was dead and has now returned to life. He was lost, but now he is found.' So the party began.

"Meanwhile, the older son was in the fields working. When he returned home, he heard music and dancing in the house, and he asked one of the servants what was going on. 'Your brother is back,' he was told, 'and your father has killed the fattened calf. We are celebrating because of his safe return.'

"The older brother was angry and wouldn't go in. His father came out and begged him, but he replied, 'All these years I've slaved for you and never once refused to do a single thing you told me to. And in all that time you never gave me even one young goat for a feast with my friends. Yet when this son of yours comes back after squandering your money on prostitutes, you celebrate by killing the fattened calf!'

"His father said to him, 'Look, dear son, you have always stayed by me, and everything I have is yours. We had to celebrate this happy day. For your brother was dead and has come back to life! He was lost, but now he is found!'"

The people in the crowd stared at Jesus in awe. They had never heard anyone describe God as a grieving father. The Scriptures were full of warnings about the wrath of God being poured out on sinners. God was scary and unapproachable. But Jesus was about to change everything. He would exchange his righteousness for our sin, to take the punishment we deserve. He would make the way for us to stand blameless before the Father forever.

As the people in the crowd turned to go home, their spirits soared, and their hearts were full of hope.

108.
Parable of the Dishonest Manager

Luke 16:1-15

When the crowd had gone, Jesus told his disciples another parable. "There was a certain rich man who had a manager handling his affairs. One day a report came that the manager was wasting his employer's money. So the employer called him in and said, 'What's this I hear about you? Get your report in order, because you are going to be fired.'

"The manager thought to himself, 'Now what? My boss has fired me. I don't have the strength to dig ditches, and I'm too proud to beg. Ah, I know how to ensure that I'll have plenty of friends who will give me a home when I am fired.'

"So he invited each person who owed money to his employer to come and discuss the situation. He asked the first one, 'How much do you owe him?' The man replied, 'I owe him 800 gallons of olive oil.' So the manager told him, 'Take the bill and quickly change it to 400 gallons.'

"'And how much do you owe my employer?' he asked the next man. 'I owe him 1,000 bushels of wheat,' was the reply. 'Here,' the manager said, 'take the bill and change it to 800 bushels.'

"The rich man had to admire the dishonest rascal for being so shrewd. And it is true that the children of this world are more shrewd in dealing with the world around them than are the children of the light. Here's the lesson: Use your worldly resources to benefit others and make friends. Then, when your possessions are gone, they will welcome you to an eternal home.

"If you are faithful in little things, you will be faithful in large ones. But if you are dishonest in little things, you won't be honest with greater responsibilities. And if you are untrustworthy about worldly wealth, who will trust you with the true riches of heaven? And if you are not faithful with other people's things, why should you be trusted with things of your own?

"No one can serve two masters. For you will hate one and love the other; you will be devoted to one and despise the other. You cannot serve God and be enslaved to money."

Some Pharisees, who loved money, had been listening in the background and they ridiculed Jesus. But he silenced them. "You like to appear righteous in public, but God knows your hearts. What this world honours is detestable in the sight of God."

109.

The Rich Man and Lazarus

Luke 16:19-31

Jesus told them another parable. "There was a certain rich man who was splendidly clothed in purple and fine linen and who lived each day in luxury. At his gate lay a poor man named Lazarus who was covered with sores. As Lazarus lay there longing for scraps from the rich man's table, the dogs would come and lick his open sores.

"Finally, the poor man died and was carried by the angels to sit beside Abraham at the heavenly banquet. The rich man also died and was buried, and he went to the place of the dead. There, in torment, he saw Abraham in the far distance with Lazarus at his side.

"The rich man shouted, 'Father Abraham, have some pity! Send Lazarus over here to dip the tip of his finger in water and cool my tongue. I am in anguish in these flames.'

"But Abraham said to him, 'Son, remember that during your lifetime you had everything you wanted, and Lazarus had nothing. So now he is here being comforted, and you are in anguish. And besides, there is a great chasm separating us. No one can cross over to you from here, and no one can cross over to us from there.'

"Then the rich man said, 'Please, Father Abraham, at least send him to my father's home. For I have five brothers, and I want him to warn them so they don't end up in this place of torment.'

"But Abraham said, 'Moses and the prophets have warned them. Your brothers can read what they wrote.'

"The rich man replied, 'No, Father Abraham! But if someone is sent to them from the dead, then they will repent of their sins and turn to God.'

"But Abraham said, 'If they won't listen to Moses and the prophets, they won't be persuaded even if someone rises from the dead.'"

110.

Servanthood

Luke 17:7-10

Jesus told the people what it meant to be a servant in the Kingdom of God. "When a servant comes in from ploughing or taking care of sheep, does his master say, 'Come in and eat with me'? No, he says, 'Prepare my meal, put on your apron, and serve me while I eat. Then you can eat later.' And does the master thank the servant for doing what he was told to do? Of course not. In the same way, when you obey me you should say, 'We are unworthy servants who have simply done our duty.'"

III.

Jesus Heals Ten Lepers

Luke 17:11-19

Jesus was travelling along the border between Galilee and Samaria, when he came to a small village. As he entered the village, ten men with leprosy stood at a distance. Their clothes were dirty and torn, and when they saw Jesus, they called out desperately, "Jesus, Master, have mercy on us!"

Jesus stopped and told them, "Go show yourselves to the priests."

The lepers walked away, and as they went, their leprosy disappeared. One of the men, who was a Samaritan, suddenly froze and stared down at his hands and arms. Then he turned and raced back to Jesus, shouting loudly, "Praise God!"

He threw himself face down in the dust at Jesus' feet and thanked him over and over again. Jesus smiled down at the man and said, "Didn't I heal ten men? Where are the other nine? Has no one returned to give glory to God except this foreigner?"

He took the Samaritan man's hands and helped him to his feet. "Stand up and go. Your faith has healed you."

112.

Parable of the Persistent Widow

Luke 18:1-8

Jesus told his disciples a parable to encourage them that they should never lose hope and never give up praying. "There was a judge in a certain city," he said, "who neither feared God nor cared about people. A widow of that city came to him repeatedly, saying, 'Give me justice in this dispute with my enemy.' The judge ignored her for a while, but finally he said to himself, 'I don't fear God or care about people, but this woman is driving me crazy. I'm going to see that she gets justice, because she is wearing me out with her constant requests!'"

Jesus looked around at his twelve men. "Learn a lesson from this unjust judge. Even he rendered a just decision in the end. So don't you think God will surely give justice to his chosen people who cry out to him day and night? Will he keep putting them off? I tell you, he will grant justice to them quickly! But when the Son of Man returns, how many will he find on the earth who have faith?"

113.

Parable of the Pharisee and the Tax Collector

Luke 18:9-14

One day Jesus was speaking to a group of people who were confident in their own righteousness. They thought they were better than everybody else, and they proudly looked down on the people around them. Jesus challenged them with a parable.

"Two men went to the Temple to pray. One was a Pharisee, and the other was a despised tax collector. The Pharisee stood by himself and prayed this prayer: 'I thank you, God, that I am not like other people - cheaters, sinners, adulterers. I'm certainly not like that tax collector! I fast twice a week, and I give you a tenth of my income.'

"But the tax collector stood at a distance and dared not even lift his eyes to heaven as he prayed. Instead, he beat his chest in sorrow, saying, 'O God, be merciful to me, for I am a sinner.' I tell you, this sinner, not the Pharisee, returned home justified before God. For those who exalt themselves will be humbled, and those who humble themselves will be exalted."

The self-righteous people scoffed and turned away. They knew the law and they thought they were good enough to earn their own righteousness by the things they did. But they were wrong. They didn't realise they could never be good enough to please God on their own. Their pride and their sin would always keep them separated from Him. Only humble faith in Jesus and complete surrender would ever be enough to make a person righteous and worthy of the Kingdom of God.

114.

Jesus Raises Lazarus from the Dead

John 11:1-44

Back in the town of Bethany, Mary and Martha were anxious. Their brother Lazarus was extremely sick and was getting worse with each day that passed. They sent a message to Jesus, saying, "Lord, your dear friend is very sick."

Jesus loved Lazarus and his sisters very much, but when he heard their message he did not go to them. All he said was, "Lazarus's sickness will not end in death. No, it happened for the glory of God so that the Son of God will receive glory from this."

Two days passed before Jesus finally told his disciples it was time to go back to Judea.

"Rabbi," they protested, "only a few days ago the people in Judea were trying to stone you. Are you going there again?"

Jesus replied, "There are twelve hours of daylight every day. During the day people can walk safely. They can see because they have the light of this world. But at night there is danger of stumbling because they have no light."

The disciples stared dumbly at Jesus, so he explained, "Our friend Lazarus has fallen asleep, but now I will go and wake him up."

The disciples thought Jesus meant Lazarus was having a good rest and he would feel better when he woke up. But Jesus told them bluntly, "Lazarus is dead. And for your sakes, I'm glad I wasn't there, for now you will really believe. Come, let's go see him."

By the time they arrived at Bethany, Lazarus had been in the grave for four days. When Martha heard that Jesus was coming, she ran to meet him outside the village. Her heart was heavy with grief and she was exhausted. "Lord, if only you had been here, my brother would not have died. But even now I know that God will give you whatever you ask."

"Your brother will rise again."

Martha sighed, "Yes, he will rise when everyone else rises, at the last day."

Jesus studied Martha carefully, and told her, "I am the resurrection and the life. Anyone who believes in me will live, even after dying. Everyone who lives in me and believes in me will never ever die. Do you believe this, Martha?"

"Yes, Lord," she replied, "I have always believed you are the Messiah, the Son of God, the one who has come into the world from God."

Martha went back to the house and pulled Mary aside so the other mourners would not overhear. "The Teacher is here and wants to see you."

Mary's eyes opened wide and her pulse quickened as she rushed out of the house. The mourners thought she was going to Lazarus's grave to weep, so they followed her to give her comfort. But Mary didn't go to the grave. She ran blindly to Jesus and fell at his feet. "Lord, if only you had been here, my brother would not have died."

Jesus looked down at Mary as she wept uncontrollably. As if on cue, the mourners began to wail in anguish. Jesus groaned in his spirit as they grew louder and louder, and his heart twisted in a painful mixture of anger and despair.

"Where have you put him?" he asked the sisters.

They took him to Lazarus' tomb. As Jesus stared at the great big stone that covered the entrance, his face suddenly crumpled and he began to weep.

Some people who were standing nearby whispered to one another, "See how much he loved him!"

But others murmured, "This man healed a blind man. Couldn't he have kept Lazarus from dying?"

Jesus groaned in his spirit again. "Roll the stone aside,"

Martha protested, "Lord, he has been dead for four days. The smell will be terrible."

Jesus looked her in the eyes and replied evenly, "Didn't I tell you that you would see God's glory if you believe?"

Martha blinked and stood back. As the stone was rolled away, Jesus looked to heaven. "Father, thank you for hearing me. You always hear me, but I said it out loud for the sake of all these people standing here, so that they will believe you sent me."

He suddenly cried out with a loud voice, "Lazarus, come out!"

Martha's jaw hung open in shock as she saw movement in the darkness. Then Lazarus walked out from the grave, still wrapped in strips of linen and with a cloth bound around his face. Tears of joy poured down Mary's cheeks as Jesus told them, "Unwrap him and let him go!"

115.

The Plot to Kill Jesus

John 11:45-57

From the moment Lazarus walked out of the grave, the atmosphere in Bethany was electric. It was all the people could talk about. Across the town, they excitedly retold the story over and over and over again. Most of the people who had witnessed the miracle believed in Jesus, but others ran straight to the Pharisees to tell them what had happened. The leading priests and the Pharisees immediately called an emergency meeting of the high council.

"What are we going to do?" they asked one another. "This man certainly performs many miraculous signs. If we allow him to go on like this, soon everyone will believe in him. Then the Roman army will come and destroy both our Temple and our nation."

An anxious murmur spread across the room and the leaders nodded.

Caiaphas, the high priest, had had enough. He stood up and hissed, "You don't know what you're talking about! You don't realise that it's better for you that one man should die for the people than for the whole nation to be destroyed."

The words came from Caiaphas' mouth, but God put them there. As the high priest, Caiaphas' words were a prophesy that Jesus would die for the entire nation. And not only for the people of Israel. His death and resurrection would cause all the children of God, scattered throughout the world, to join together.

From that moment on, the Jewish leaders began to plot the death of Jesus. So Jesus left Bethany and went out near the wilderness, to a village called Ephraim, and he stayed there with his disciples.

Meanwhile, it was almost time for the Passover festival. The Jews began to flood into Jerusalem from every direction and there was only one name on their lips: Jesus! They looked for him wherever they went and as they stood in the Temple courts, they asked one another, "What do you think? He won't come for Passover, will he?"

The leading priests and the Pharisees were also looking for Jesus, and they put out a public order: Anyone who saw him was to report him immediately so they could arrest him.

116.

Jesus Predicts His Death a Third Time

Matthew 20:17-19,
Mark 10:32-34, Luke 18:31-34

The disciples were in low spirits as they followed Jesus along the road to Jerusalem. Nobody said a word, and their hearts were full of apprehension. They all knew the Pharisees and religious leaders were after Jesus, and they could not work out why he would risk going to the Passover.

Jesus stopped and waited for his disciples to catch up. Then he pulled them aside, away from the crowd. He told them in detail everything that was going to happen to him.

"Listen, we're going up to Jerusalem, where all the predictions of the prophets concerning the Son of Man will come true. He will be betrayed to the leading priests and the teachers of religious law. They will sentence him to die and hand him over to the Romans. They will mock him, spit on him, flog him with a whip, and kill him, but after three days he will rise again."

The disciples stared at Jesus in silence. He had said it as plainly as he could, but still the full meaning of his words was hidden from them.

Jesus turned and set his face towards Jerusalem for the final time.

117.

Greatness is Serving

Matthew 20:20-28, Mark 10:35-45

James and John had been talking in hushed voices as they walked along. Now they nudged each other forward, and both fell into step beside Jesus.

"Teacher," John began hesitantly, "we want you to do us a favour."

Jesus looked sideways at the two brothers. "What is your request?"

James answered quietly, so the other disciples wouldn't hear, "When you sit on your glorious throne, we want to sit in places of honour next to you, one on your right and the other on your left."

They looked expectantly at Jesus. But Jesus frowned. "You don't know what you are asking! Are you able to drink from the bitter cup of suffering

I am about to drink? Are you able to be baptised with the baptism of suffering I must be baptised with?"

"Oh yes," they nodded seriously, "we are able!"

Jesus shook his head and looked them in the eyes, "You will indeed drink from my bitter cup and be baptised with my baptism of suffering. But I have no right to say who will sit on my right or my left. God has prepared those places for the ones he has chosen."

The other ten disciples were indignant when they heard what James and John had requested. Jesus gathered them all around and told them, "You know that the rulers in this world lord it over their people, and officials flaunt their authority over those under them. But among you it will be different. Whoever wants to be a leader among you must be your servant, and whoever wants to be first among you must be the slave of everyone else. For even the Son of Man came not to be served but to serve others and to give his life as a ransom for many."

The disciples were silent as they continued on their way to Jerusalem.

118.

Jesus and Zacchaeus

Luke 19:1-10

Zacchaeus was desperate to see Jesus as he passed through Jericho. But the streets were full of people, and no matter how much he pushed and jostled, Zacchaeus could not get through the crowd. He ducked and he shoved, but it was no use. He was too short to see anything. To make matters worse, the people scowled at him and blocked his view on purpose. They all knew who he was. He was the chief tax collector in the area, and that made him a liar and a cheat.

Finally, Zacchaeus had an idea. He ran down the road and climbed a tall sycamore tree. From there he could see everything, and he watched as Jesus made his way through the city. When Jesus came to the tree, he stopped. Zacchaeus almost fell off his branch when Jesus looked up and called him by name.

"Zacchaeus! Quick, come down! I must be a guest in your home today."

Zacchaeus scrambled down in surprise. Then he proudly led Jesus through the streets towards his home. The people in the crowd watched them go, and they grumbled in disgust. "He has gone to be the guest of a notorious sinner."

They were right. Zacchaeus had done many terrible things. When men lost their farms, and families were torn apart because they couldn't pay their taxes, he didn't care. He just got richer.

But now, as Jesus stood in his luxurious home, Zacchaeus felt ashamed of the things he had done. At that moment, he realised that Jesus loved sinners, regardless of how bad they had been. Zacchaeus was overcome with humility and suddenly nothing else in his life mattered. Not the money, not the luxury, not the fine clothes or the prestige.

He felt pure exhilaration as he told Jesus, "I will give half my wealth to the poor, Lord, and if I have cheated people on their taxes, I will give them back four times as much!"

Jesus smiled and clapped Zacchaeus on the shoulder. "Salvation has come to this home today, for this man has shown himself to be a true son of Abraham. For the Son of Man came to seek and save those who are lost."

119.

Blind Bartimaeus

Matthew 20:29-33,
Mark 10:46-52, Luke 18:35-43

The crowd spilled out of Jericho and followed Jesus along the road. A blind man named Bartimaeus, was begging in his usual spot by the roadside. When he heard all the commotion, he asked the people around him what was going on. They told him that Jesus of Nazareth was passing by.

Bartimaeus immediately sat upright and began to shout, "Jesus, Son of David, have mercy on me!"

The people next to him shushed him and told him to be quiet. But he only yelled louder and louder. "Son of David, have mercy on me!"

Jesus stopped walking and called Bartimaeus to come.

The same people who had shushed him, turned to him excitedly. "Cheer up," they said. "Come on, he's calling you!"

Bartimaeus threw off his beggar's coat and shuffled towards Jesus.

"What do you want me to do for you?" Jesus asked.

Bartimaeus scrunched up his face. "My Rabbi, I want to see!"

Jesus told him, "Go, for your faith has healed you."

At that moment Bartimaeus could see, and he stared in awe at the people around him. He looked at the trees along the road and the gravel under his feet. Then he laughed and laughed. Bartimaeus joined the crowd as they praised God and followed Jesus along the road to Jerusalem.

120.

Parable of the Three Servants

Matthew 25:14-30, Luke 19:11-27

Jesus stopped walking and waited for the crowd to gather around. Jerusalem was not far away, and the people still had the wrong idea of who he was and why he had come. They thought the Kingdom of God was going to begin immediately and that Jesus would soon sit on the throne. But Jesus would not be confined to an earthly throne in a single city. Instead, the Kingdom of God would be an invisible kingdom, represented in the hearts of his people. Jesus would return to heaven and leave his followers to carry on his mission. But one day he would return in his glory and in the glory of his Father and establish his reign.

Jesus told them a parable to explain: "The Kingdom of Heaven can be illustrated by the story of a man going on a long trip. He called together his servants and entrusted his money to them while he was gone. He gave five bags of silver to one, two bags of silver to another, and one bag of silver to the last - dividing it in proportion to their abilities. He then left on his trip.

"The servant who received the five bags of silver began to invest the money and earned five more. The servant with two bags of silver also went to work and earned two more. But the servant who received the one bag of silver dug a hole in the ground and hid the master's money.

"After a long time their master returned from his trip and called them to give an account of how they had used his money. The servant to whom he had entrusted the five bags of silver came forward with five more and said, 'Master, you gave me five bags of silver to invest, and I have earned five more.'

"The master was full of praise. 'Well done, my good and faithful servant. You have been faithful in handling this small amount, so now I will give you many more responsibilities. Let's celebrate together!'

"The servant who had received the two bags of silver came forward and said, 'Master, you gave me two bags of silver to invest, and I have earned two more.'

"The master said, 'Well done, my good and faithful servant. You have been faithful in handling this small amount, so now I will give you many more responsibilities. Let's celebrate together!'

"Then the servant with the one bag of silver came and said, 'Master, I knew you were a harsh man, harvesting crops you didn't plant and gathering crops you didn't cultivate. I was afraid I would lose your money, so I hid it in the earth. Look, here is your money back.'

"But the master replied, 'You wicked and lazy servant! If you knew I harvested crops I didn't plant and gathered crops I didn't cultivate, why didn't you deposit my money in the bank? At least I could have gotten some interest on it.'

"Then he ordered, 'Take the money from this servant, and give it to the one with the ten bags of silver. To those who use well what they are given, even more will be given, and they will have an abundance. But from those who do nothing, even what little they have will be taken away. Now throw this useless servant into outer darkness, where there will be weeping and gnashing of teeth.'

121.

The Triumphal Entry

Matthew 21:1-11, Mark 11:1-10,
Luke 19:28-40, John 12:12-19

Jesus had reached the Mount of Olives, and Jerusalem was only three kilometres away. He called two of his disciples over and spoke to them quietly.

"Go into that village over there," he told them. "As soon as you enter it, you will see a young donkey tied there that no one has ever ridden. Untie it and bring it here. If anyone asks, 'What are you doing?' just say, 'The Lord needs it and will return it soon.'"

The two disciples went into the village and found the colt just as Jesus had said. As they were untying it, some people came out and demanded, "What are you doing, untying that colt?"

The disciples looked at each other, and hesitantly replied, "The Lord needs it."

The people agreed to let them take the animal, and they led it back to Jesus. Then they laid their cloaks over its back for Jesus to sit on.

Meanwhile, the news that Jesus was on his way into Jerusalem spread quickly. Thousands of Passover visitors cut palm branches and went out along the road to meet him. This was the moment they had all been waiting for. The Messiah was coming! They laid their robes and palm branches on the road for him and waited in anticipation to honour their new conquering king.

For three years Jesus had rejected any praise that was directed at him. He had avoided publicity and slipped away from the crowds when they grew too large. When he healed people, he had told them not to tell anybody. And when demons recognised him, he had not let them speak. But now, as he began his descent down the Mount of Olives towards Jerusalem, the people erupted. They waved palm branches in the air, they shouted and sang and cheered. "Praise God! Blessings on the one who comes in the name of the Lord! Hail to the King of Israel!"

And Jesus let them shout. For his hour had come.

The disciples didn't recognise it at the time, but later on, after Jesus had entered his glory, they would remember the words of the prophet Zechariah:

"Don't be afraid, people of Jerusalem.
Look, your King is coming,
 riding on a donkey's colt."

The Pharisees stared at the triumphant crowd in horror. "Teacher, rebuke your followers for saying things like that!"

But as Jesus passed them, he replied, "If they kept quiet, the stones along the road would burst into cheers!"

The Pharisees were dumbfounded, and they said to one another, "There's nothing we can do. Look, everyone has gone after him!"

122.

Jesus Weeps for Jerusalem

Luke 19:41-44

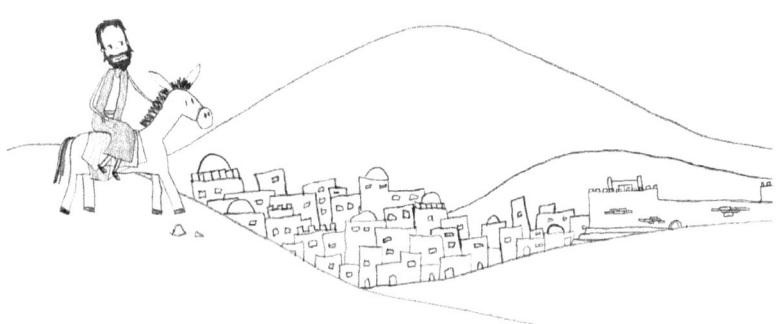

The people adored Jesus. They were ready to crown their king. But as they waved their palm branches and praised the God of Israel, Jesus' thoughts were far away. His gaze swept over the magnificent city of Jerusalem, sprawled out before him in all its glory. Jesus was suddenly overcome with emotion and he began to weep.

He wept for the people of Jerusalem. For those who refused to repent and turn away from their sin. For those who would not accept him as their Lord and Saviour. He wept for the people in the crowd who shouted his praise. In a few short days those same people would be demanding his death. And he wept for the suffering that would soon overwhelm the city and everyone in it.

Jesus' voice cracked, "How I wish today that you of all people would understand the way to peace. But now it is too late, and peace is hidden from your eyes. Before long your enemies will build ramparts against your walls and encircle you and close in on you from every side. They will crush you into the ground, and your children with you. Your enemies will not leave a single stone in place, because you did not recognise it when God visited you."

Sure enough, forty years later, Titus and the Roman army would surround the great city of Jerusalem, trapping the people inside and cutting off all their supplies. The city would be completely destroyed, and the Temple would be torn down and burned to the ground. It would never be rebuilt. The Jews who did not escape would be killed by the tens of thousands. Others would be taken as slaves or sent to the gladiator arena to entertain the Roman crowd. Jesus could see what was coming, and it broke his heart.

123.

Jesus is Anointed at Bethany

Matthew 26:6-13, Mark 14:3-9, John 12:1-11

Hundreds of thousands of people had crowded into Jerusalem and the surrounding villages for the Passover. The festival would last for a whole week, and every house was overflowing with guests. Even the hills that bordered the city were dotted with tents and campfires that burned into the night.

Over in the town of Bethany, Jesus reclined at the table while Martha served a special meal to honour him. Everybody fell silent as Mary quietly entered the room. It was the first time she had seen Jesus since her brother,

Lazarus, had been raised from the dead. She knelt beside Jesus with a shy smile. In her hands she cradled a twelve-ounce jar of perfume made from pure nard. Without a word, she broke the jar open and poured the perfume over Jesus' head. As the musky fragrance filled the air, some of the disciples frowned. Judas Iscariot made an ugly face and objected loudly, "That perfume was worth a year's wages. It should have been sold and the money given to the poor."

Judas sounded like he cared about the needy, but he was in fact a thief. He was in charge of the disciples' moneybag and had been stealing from it the whole time. Mary stood up quickly, her eyes wide and her face turning red with embarrassment. But Jesus smiled and took her hand. "Leave her alone. Why criticise her for doing such a good thing to me? You will always have the poor among you, and you can help them whenever you want to. But you will not always have me. She has done what she could and has anointed my body for burial ahead of time. I tell you the truth, wherever the Good News is preached throughout the world, this woman's deed will be remembered and discussed."

124.

Jesus Curses the Fig Tree

Matthew 21:18-22, Mark 11:12-14, 11:20-25

Early the next morning Jesus and his disciples made their way down to Jerusalem. Jesus was feeling hungry when he noticed a fig tree growing beside the road. The tree was full of leaves, but there was not one fig on it because it was not the right season. Jesus studied the tree, and then suddenly cursed it, "May you never bear fruit again!"

To the disciples' amazement, the fig tree immediately withered up and died.

"How did the fig tree wither so quickly?" they exclaimed as they stared at the tree in awe.

Jesus answered, "I tell you the truth, if you have faith and don't doubt, you can do things like this and much more. You can even say to this mountain, 'May you be lifted up and thrown into the sea,' and it will happen. But you must really believe it will happen and have no doubt in your heart. I tell you, you can pray for anything, and if you believe that you've received it, it will be yours. But when you are praying, first forgive anyone you are holding a grudge against, so that your Father in heaven will forgive your sins, too."

125.

Jesus Clears the Temple Again

Matthew 21:12-17,
Mark 11:15-19, Luke 19:45-46

The Temple courts were crowded with pilgrims who had made the journey to Jerusalem. Jesus moved along with them, taking in every detail and growing more and more agitated with every step. Three years had passed since he cleared the Temple the first time, and nothing had changed. The merchants and the money changers still sat at their tables. Every Jew or foreigner who came to worship God was ripped off again and again. The religious leaders were so out of tune with God, and so consumed with their own comfort and power, that they saw nothing wrong with it. Jesus gritted his teeth. God's house was a thriving marketplace, and he couldn't stand it.

The people in the crowd turned and stared as Jesus began to drive out every person who was buying and selling. Once again, he threw over the money changer's tables and upended the benches of the people selling pigeons. Coins and feathers flew everywhere, and Jesus' booming voice ricocheted off the walls. "The Scriptures declare, 'My Temple will be called a house of prayer for all nations,' but you have turned it into a den of thieves."

As the people stared at Jesus in stunned silence, something amazing happened. A blind man fumbled his way through the crowd towards him. A lame man shuffled closely behind. One by one, people with all kinds of physical deformities and illnesses came out from the crowd until they surrounded Jesus. He touched each one of them and they were healed.

The leading priests and the teachers of religious law were furious. As they pushed their way through the crowd, they heard some children joyfully shouting, "Praise God for the Son of David!"

That was the last straw. In a furious rage, they turned on Jesus, "Do you hear what these children are saying?"

"Yes," Jesus replied, his eyes burning. "Haven't you ever read the Scriptures? For they say, 'You have taught children and infants to give you praise.'"

Jesus left the Temple and returned to Bethany with his disciples.

126.
The Authority of Jesus Challenged

Matthew 21:23-32,
Mark 11:27-33, Luke 19:47-20:8

Jesus continued to teach at the Temple every day. The leading priests, teachers of religious law and the elders were desperate to destroy him, but there was nothing they could do because the people hung on every word he said. The religious leaders could not deny the authority with which Jesus spoke, any more than they could explain his miraculous signs. But they were furious that this untrained, self-appointed rabbi could hold so much influence over the people, and even challenge them in their own Temple.

The leading priests and teachers of religious law, along with the elders, approached Jesus and demanded, "By what authority are you doing all these things? Who gave you the right?"

Jesus had never backed down from any confrontation and these self-righteous men would never intimidate him. He looked them squarely in the eyes, and replied, "I'll tell you by what authority I do these things if you answer one question. Did John's authority to baptise come from heaven, or was it merely human?"

The religious leaders frowned and looked at one another. Then they huddled together to talk it over. They realised too late that Jesus had caught them in their own trap. "If we say it was from heaven, he will ask us why we didn't believe John. But if we say it was merely human, we'll be mobbed because the people believe John was a prophet."

The men glowered at Jesus as they finally answered, "We don't know."

Jesus shook his head and said, "Then I won't tell you by what authority I do these things. But what do you think about this? A man with two sons told the older boy, 'Son, go out and work in the vineyard today.' The son answered, 'No, I won't go,' but later he changed his mind and went anyway. Then the father told the other son, 'You go,' and he said, 'Yes, sir, I will.' But he didn't go. Which of the two obeyed his father?"

The priests and leaders replied, "The first one, of course."

Then Jesus explained the meaning of the parable to them: Doing something is more important than simply saying something. "I tell you the truth, corrupt tax collectors and prostitutes will get into the Kingdom of God before you do. For John the Baptist came and showed you the right way to live, but you didn't believe him, while tax collectors and prostitutes did. And even when you saw this happening, you refused to believe him and repent of your sins."

127.

Parable of the Evil Farmers

Matthew 21:33-46,
Mark 12:1-12, Luke 20:9-19

The religious leaders were seething, but Jesus had another parable for them. "A man planted a vineyard. He built a wall around it, dug a pit for pressing out the grape juice, and built a lookout tower. Then he leased the vineyard to tenant farmers and moved to another country. At the time of the grape harvest, he sent one of his servants to collect his share of the crop. But the farmers grabbed the servant, beat him up, and sent him back empty-handed. The owner then sent another servant, but they insulted him and beat him over the head. The next servant he sent was killed. Others he sent were either beaten or killed, until there was only one left - his son whom he loved dearly. The owner finally sent him, thinking, 'Surely they will respect my son.'

"But the tenant farmers said to one another, 'Here comes the heir to this estate. Let's kill him and get the estate for ourselves!' So they grabbed him and murdered him and threw his body out of the vineyard. When the owner of the vineyard returns, what do you think he will do to those farmers?"

The priests and leaders replied angrily, "He will put the wicked men to a horrible death and lease the vineyard to others who will give him his share of the crop after each harvest."

Jesus gazed sadly at the men. They had answered correctly, but they were so blind. They could not see that they themselves were the evil farmers in the parable. The servants were the prophets of Israel who had been rejected and killed as they warned the people to repent of their sin and turn back to God. And now Israel was rejecting God's own Son.

Jesus asked them, "Didn't you ever read this in the Scriptures?

'The stone that the builders rejected
   has now become the cornerstone.
This is the Lord's doing,
   and it is wonderful to see.'"

The people in the crowd were staring blankly at Jesus, so he explained the parable to them. "I tell you, the Kingdom of God will be taken away from you and given to a nation that will produce the proper fruit. Anyone who stumbles over that stone will be broken to pieces, and it will crush anyone it falls on."

The religious leaders suddenly realised the parable was about them. They were the wicked farmers. They clenched their teeth in fury and glared at Jesus. They wanted to arrest him right there, but they knew the people would start a riot if they laid a single finger on him.

128.

The Wedding Banquet

Matthew 22:1-14, Luke 14:15-24

Jesus looked the religious leaders in the eyes and told them one last parable. "The Kingdom of Heaven can be illustrated by the story of a king who prepared a great wedding feast for his son. When the banquet was ready, he sent his servant to tell the guests, 'Come, the banquet is ready.' But they all began making excuses. One said, 'I have just bought a field and must inspect it. Please excuse me.' Another said, 'I have just bought five pairs of oxen, and I want to try them out. Please excuse me.' Another said, 'I just got married, so I can't come.'

"The servant returned and told his master what they had said. His master was furious and said, 'Go quickly into the streets and alleys of the town and invite the poor, the crippled, the blind, and the lame.' After the servant had done this, he reported, 'There is still room for more.' So his master said, 'Go out into the country lanes and behind the hedges and urge anyone you find to come, so that the house will be full. For none of those I first invited will get even the smallest taste of my banquet.'

"So the servants brought in everyone they could find, good and bad alike, and the banquet hall was filled with guests."

Jesus paused to let the parable sink in. "But when the king came in to meet the guests, he noticed a man who wasn't wearing the proper clothes for a wedding. 'Friend,' he asked, 'how is it that you are here without wedding clothes?' But the man had no reply. Then the king said to his aides, 'Bind his hands and feet and throw him into the outer darkness, where there will be weeping and gnashing of teeth.' For many are called, but few are chosen."

The priests and religious leaders stared at Jesus as the meaning of the parable became staggeringly clear. God had told Abraham two thousand years earlier that every nation on earth would be blessed through his descendants. And now, because God's chosen nation, Israel, would not recognise Jesus as the Messiah and would reject his invitation into the Kingdom of Heaven, God would extend the invitation to all of mankind. The Kingdom of God would belong to people from every tribe and nation, of every colour and every language.

129.

The Son of Man Must Be Lifted Up

John 12:20-36

A group of Greek travellers were in Jerusalem to worship during the Passover. They had heard of the miraculous things Jesus was doing and were interested in his teaching. They had asked Philip if they could meet with Jesus, and Philip had taken them to Andrew. Now Andrew and Philip snaked their way through the crowd to find Jesus.

When Jesus heard their request, he looked out at all the foreigners scattered throughout the crowd. In a few short days it wouldn't matter whether they were Jew or Gentile, slave or free, male or female. Every person who believed in Jesus would be united through him. Salvation would be available to everyone.

Jesus looked back at Andrew and Philip. "Now the time has come for the Son of Man to enter into his glory."

A ripple of excitement shot through the crowd. This was it. They could finally crown their king. But the glory Jesus meant was not the glory they were expecting. "I tell you the truth, unless a kernel of wheat is planted in the soil and dies, it remains alone. But its death will produce many new kernels - a plentiful harvest of new lives. Those who love their life in this world will lose it. Those who care nothing for their life in this world will keep it for eternity. Anyone who wants to serve me must follow me, because my servants must be where I am. And the Father will honour anyone who serves me."

The people in the crowd stared at Jesus expectantly as he continued. "Now my soul is deeply troubled. Should I pray, 'Father, save me from this hour'? But this is the very reason I came! Father, bring glory to your name."

As Jesus finished speaking, a voice suddenly came from heaven. "I have already brought glory to my name, and I will do so again."

Everybody in the crowd looked around, confused. Some of them thought the voice had thundered down, while others were sure an angel had spoken.

Jesus told them, "The voice was for your benefit, not mine. The time for judging this world has come, when Satan, the ruler of this world, will be cast out. And when I am lifted up from the earth, I will draw everyone to myself."

The people frowned and scratched their heads. "We understood from Scripture that the Messiah would live forever. How can you say the Son of Man will die? Just who is this Son of Man, anyway?"

The people were so confused. How could a king rule when he was dead? They didn't understand that Jesus' Kingdom would not be an earthly kingdom. Earthly kingdoms come and go, and earthly rulers die. But Jesus' Kingdom will never pass away or be conquered by any other.

Jesus looked at the crowd intently. "My light will shine for you just a little longer. Walk in the light while you can, so the darkness will not overtake you. Those who walk in the darkness cannot see where they are going. Put your trust in the light while there is still time; then you will become children of the light."

When he finished speaking, Jesus left and hid himself away from the crowds.

130.

The Unbelief of the People

John 12:37-50

All over Jerusalem people were talking about one man. Jesus. In every house, on every street corner and all through the marketplace, the people talked and argued about him. Despite the miraculous signs and all the amazing things Jesus had done, most people still did not believe in him.

Seven hundred years earlier the prophet Isaiah had said:

"Lord, who has believed our message?
  To whom has the Lord revealed his powerful arm?"

But the people couldn't believe, for as Isaiah also said,

"The Lord has blinded their eyes
    and hardened their hearts -
so that their eyes cannot see,
    and their hearts cannot understand,
and they cannot turn to me
    and have me heal them."

The debate about Jesus raged on and on. Many people did believe in him, including many Jewish leaders. But they did not dare to admit it in public. They were afraid if they did, the Pharisees would ban them from the synagogues, and their reputations would be ruined. Sadly, they preferred the praise of people more than the praise of God, and they were unwilling to give up their status and position to follow Jesus.

Jesus knew how divided the people were. He cried out, "If you trust me, you are trusting not only me, but also God who sent me. For when you see me, you are seeing the one who sent me. I have come as a light to shine in this dark world, so that all who put their trust in me will no longer remain in the dark. I will not judge those who hear me but don't obey me, for I have come to save the world and not to judge it. But all who reject me and my message will be judged on the day of judgment by the truth I have spoken. I don't speak on my own authority. The Father who sent me has commanded me what to say and how to say it. And I know his commands lead to eternal life; so I say whatever the Father tells me to say."

131.

The Leaders Try to Trap Jesus

Matthew 22:15-33,
Mark 12:13-27, Luke 20:20-40

The religious leaders were desperate to arrest Jesus, so they called a secret meeting and came up with a plan. They would send some of their own disciples as spies to try to trick him. All they needed to do was get Jesus to say something that could be used against him, then they could report him to the Roman governor, and he would be arrested.

The spies went straight to Jesus.

"Teacher," they began, "we know that you speak and teach what is right and are not influenced by what others think. You teach the way of God truthfully. Now tell us - is it right for us to pay taxes to Caesar or not?"

Jesus saw right through their flattery and knew what their motives were. If he answered no, the religious leaders would take him to the governor and charge him with treason against Rome. But if he said yes, they would accuse him of disloyalty to the Jewish nation.

"You hypocrites!" he said. "Why are you trying to trap me? Show me a Roman coin. Whose picture and title are stamped on it?"

"Caesar's," they replied, holding out a denarius for Jesus to see.

"Well then," he said, "give to Caesar what belongs to Caesar, and give to God what belongs to God."

The spies looked at one another in surprise and did not know how to respond. As they sank back into the crowd some Sadducees stepped forward. They were also eager to trap Jesus.

The Sadducees didn't believe in resurrection or life after death, so they asked Jesus, "Teacher, Moses gave us a law that if a man dies, leaving a wife without children, his brother should marry the widow and have a child who will carry on the brother's name. Well, suppose there were seven brothers. The oldest one married and then died without children. So the second brother married the widow, but he also died without children. Then the third brother married her. This continued with all seven of them, and still there were no children. Last of all, the woman also died. So tell us, whose wife will she be in the resurrection? For all seven were married to her."

Jesus shook his head as he replied, "Your mistake is that you don't know the Scriptures, and you don't know the power of God. For when the dead rise, they will neither marry nor be given in marriage. In this respect they will be like the angels in heaven.

"But now, as to whether the dead will be raised - haven't you ever read about this in the writings of Moses, in the story of the burning bush? Long after Abraham, Isaac, and Jacob had died, God said to Moses, 'I am the God of Abraham, the God of Isaac, and the God of Jacob.' So he is the God of the living, not the dead. You have made a serious error."

The Sadducees were silenced and everybody in the crowd was astounded by the way Jesus spoke.

132.

The Greatest Commandment

Matthew 22:34-40, Mark 12:28-34

One of the teachers of religious law had been standing nearby listening to the discussion. He was an expert in interpreting the law and was impressed by Jesus' answers. He came closer and asked, "Of all the commandments, which is the most important?"

Jesus turned to the man and replied, "The most important commandment is this: 'Listen, O Israel! The Lord our God is the one and only Lord. And you must love the Lord your God with all your heart, all your soul, all your mind, and all your strength.' The second is equally important: 'Love your neighbour as yourself.' No other commandment is greater than these."

The man nodded, "Well said, Teacher. You have spoken the truth by saying that there is only one God and no other. And I know it is important to love him with all my heart and all my understanding and all my strength, and to love my neighbour as myself. This is more important than to offer all of the burnt offerings and sacrifices required in the law."

Jesus was pleased with the man's wise answer, and told him, "You are not far from the Kingdom of God."

133.

Whose Son is the Messiah?

Matthew 22:41-46,
Mark 12:35-40, Luke 20:41-47

Jesus turned to some Pharisees who had gathered at the edge of the crowd. He had some questions of his own. "What do you think about the Messiah? Whose son is he?"

"He is the son of David," the men replied.

Their answer was obvious because the Scriptures prophesied that the Messiah would come from the descendants of King David. But Jesus wanted them to know that the Messiah was not only the son of David. He was also God.

"Then why does David, speaking under the inspiration of the Spirit, call the Messiah 'my Lord'? For David said,

'The Lord said to my Lord,
Sit in the place of honour at my right hand
   until I humble your enemies beneath your feet.'

Since David called the Messiah 'my Lord,' how can the Messiah be his son?"

The men looked at one another helplessly, but they had no reply. The rest of the crowd stayed silent, and from that day on, nobody dared to ask any more questions.

134.

The Widow's Offering

Mark 12:41-44, Luke 21:1-4

Back at the Temple, Jesus sat across from the treasury and watched as the people put their money into the offering box. Some of them kept their heads down as they dropped their coins in. Others proudly made a big show of it, so the people around them would notice the large amount they put in.

Jesus watched a poor widow move up to the box. Her hands were clasped tightly to her chest and she hovered there for a moment, her eyes closed and her lips moving in a silent prayer. She dropped two small coins into the box and then slowly shuffled away.

"I tell you the truth," Jesus said to his disciples, "this poor widow has given more than all the rest of them. For they gave a tiny part of their surplus, but she, poor as she is, has given everything she had to live on."

135.

The Coming of the Kingdom

Matthew 24:1-51, Mark 13:1-37,
Luke 12:35-48, 17:20-37, 21:5-38

As they were leaving, the disciples turned back to admire the Temple. The stone blocks that made up the walls were absolutely huge. The sun reflected off the white marble walls of the buildings and made a brilliant sight. No matter how many times they visited Jerusalem, they never grew tired of the Temple or its splendour.

"Teacher, look at these magnificent buildings! Look at the impressive stones in the walls," they exclaimed in awe.

Jesus stopped walking and looked back. Then he predicted for the second time the destruction of the great Temple. "Yes, look at these great buildings. But they will be completely demolished. Not one stone will be left on top of another!"

Later, Jesus was sitting on the Mount of Olives when four of his disciples came to see him privately. Peter, James, John and Andrew gazed across the valley as they sat down. The Temple stood so proudly above the city walls, but they couldn't stop thinking about what Jesus had said.

"Tell us, when will all this happen? What sign will show us that these things are about to be fulfilled?"

Jesus told them, "Don't let anyone mislead you, for many will come in my name, claiming, 'I am the Messiah,' and saying, 'The time has come!' But don't believe them. And when you hear of wars and insurrections, don't panic. Yes, these things must take place first, but the end won't follow immediately. Nation will go to war against nation, and kingdom against kingdom. There will be famines and earthquakes in many parts of the world. But all this is only the first of the birth pains, with more to come.

"Then you will be arrested, persecuted, and killed. You will be hated all over the world because you are my followers. And many will turn away from me and betray and hate each other. And many false prophets will appear and will deceive many people. Sin will be rampant everywhere, and the love of many will grow cold. But the one who endures to the end will be saved. And the Good News about the Kingdom will be preached throughout the whole world, so that all nations will hear it; and then the end will come."

Peter let out his breath. The other men were silent. Jesus continued, "The time is coming when you will long to see the day when the Son of Man returns, but you won't see it. People will tell you, 'Look, there is the Son of Man,' or 'Here he is,' but don't go out and follow them. For as the lightning flashes in the east and shines to the west, so it will be when the Son of Man comes. Just as the gathering of vultures shows there is a carcass nearby, so these signs indicate that the end is near.

"Immediately after the anguish of those days,
the sun will be darkened,
    the moon will give no light,
the stars will fall from the sky,
    and the powers in the heavens will be shaken.

"And then at last, the sign that the Son of Man is coming will appear in the heavens, and there will be deep mourning among all the peoples of the earth. And they will see the Son of Man coming on the clouds of heaven with power and great glory. And he will send out his angels with the mighty blast of a trumpet, and they will gather his chosen ones from all over the world - from the farthest ends of the earth and heaven."

Jesus gazed intently at his four closest friends. "When the Son of Man returns, it will be like it was in Noah's day. In those days, the people enjoyed banquets and parties and weddings right up to the time Noah entered his boat and the flood came and destroyed them all.

"And the world will be as it was in the days of Lot. People went about their daily business - eating and drinking, buying and selling, farming and building - until the morning Lot left Sodom. Then fire and burning sulfur rained down from heaven and destroyed them all. Yes, it will be 'business as usual' right up to the day when the Son of Man is revealed. On that day a person out on the deck of a roof must not go down into the house to pack. A person out in the field must not return home. Remember what happened to Lot's wife! If you cling to your life, you will lose it, and if you let your life go, you will save it. That night two people will be asleep in one bed; one will be taken, the other left. Two men will be working together in the field; one will be taken, the other left. Two women will be grinding flour at the mill; one will be taken, the other left."

The disciples were stunned. "Where will this happen, Lord?"

But Jesus replied, "No one knows the day or hour when these things will happen, not even the angels in heaven or the Son himself. Only the Father knows. And since you don't know when that time will come, be on guard! Stay alert!

"The coming of the Son of Man can be illustrated by the story of a man going on a long trip. When he left home, he gave each of his slaves instructions about the work they were to do, and he told the gatekeeper to watch for his return. You, too, must keep watch! For you don't know when the master of the household will return - in the evening, at midnight, before dawn, or at daybreak. Don't let him find you sleeping when he arrives without warning. I say to you what I say to everyone: Watch for him!

"Understand this: If a homeowner knew exactly when a burglar was coming, he would not permit his house to be broken into. You also must be ready all the time, for the Son of Man will come when least expected."

Peter frowned. "Lord, is that illustration just for us or for everyone?"

Jesus told him, "A faithful, sensible servant is one to whom the master can give the responsibility of managing his other household servants and feeding them. If the master returns and finds that the servant has done a good job, there will be a reward. I tell you the truth, the master will put that servant in charge of all he owns. But what if the servant thinks, 'My master won't be back for a while,' and he begins beating the other servants, partying, and getting drunk? The master will return unannounced and unexpected, and he will cut the servant in pieces and banish him with the unfaithful.

"And a servant who knows what the master wants, but isn't prepared and doesn't carry out those instructions, will be severely punished. But someone who does not know, and then does something wrong, will be punished only lightly. When someone has been given much, much will be required in return; and when someone has been entrusted with much, even more will be required."

136.

Parable of the Ten Bridesmaids

Matthew 25:1-13

"The Kingdom of Heaven will be like ten bridesmaids who took their lamps and went to meet the bridegroom. Five of them were foolish, and five were wise. The five who were foolish didn't take enough olive oil for their lamps, but the other five were wise enough to take along extra oil. When the bridegroom was delayed, they all became drowsy and fell asleep.

"At midnight they were roused by the shout, 'Look, the bridegroom is coming! Come out and meet him!'

"All the bridesmaids got up and prepared their lamps. Then the five foolish ones asked the others, 'Please give us some of your oil because our lamps are going out.'

"But the others replied, 'We don't have enough for all of us. Go to a shop and buy some for yourselves.'

"But while they were gone to buy oil, the bridegroom came. Then those who were ready went in with him to the marriage feast, and the door was locked. Later, when the other five bridesmaids returned, they stood outside, calling, 'Lord! Lord! Open the door for us!'

"But he called back, 'Believe me, I don't know you!'

"So you, too, must keep watch! For you do not know the day or hour of my return."

137.

The Final Judgment

Matthew 25:31-46, 26:1-2

"But when the Son of Man comes in his glory, and all the angels with him, then he will sit upon his glorious throne. All the nations will be gathered in his presence, and he will separate the people as a shepherd separates the sheep from the goats. He will place the sheep at his right hand and the goats at his left.

"Then the King will say to those on his right, 'Come, you who are blessed by my Father, inherit the Kingdom prepared for you from the creation of the world. For I was hungry, and you fed me. I was thirsty, and you gave me a drink. I was a stranger, and you invited me into your home.

I was naked, and you gave me clothing. I was sick, and you cared for me. I was in prison, and you visited me.'

"Then these righteous ones will reply, 'Lord, when did we ever see you hungry and feed you? Or thirsty and give you something to drink? Or a stranger and show you hospitality? Or naked and give you clothing? When did we ever see you sick or in prison and visit you?'

"And the King will say, 'I tell you the truth, when you did it to one of the least of these my brothers and sisters, you were doing it to me!'

"Then the King will turn to those on the left and say, 'Away with you, you cursed ones, into the eternal fire prepared for the devil and his demons. For I was hungry, and you didn't feed me. I was thirsty, and you didn't give me a drink. I was a stranger, and you didn't invite me into your home. I was naked, and you didn't give me clothing. I was sick and in prison, and you didn't visit me.'

"Then they will reply, 'Lord, when did we ever see you hungry or thirsty or a stranger or naked or sick or in prison, and not help you?'

"And he will answer, 'I tell you the truth, when you refused to help the least of these my brothers and sisters, you were refusing to help me.'

"And they will go away into eternal punishment, but the righteous will go into eternal life."

Jesus paused and studied his hands. His time was running out. When he looked up, his disciples were staring at him and he met their eyes one at a time as he spoke. "As you know, Passover begins in two days, and the Son of Man will be handed over to be crucified."

138.

Judas and the Plot to Kill Jesus

Matthew 26:1-5 & 26:14-16,
Mark 14:1-2, 14:10-11, Luke 22:1-6

At that very moment, the leading priests and the teachers of religious law were gathering at the home of Caiaphas, the high priest. They had called a secret meeting to discuss once and for all what to do with Jesus. From the moment he began preaching, he had offended them and steadily chipped away at their rules and religion. They had tried to reason with him. They had tried to intimidate and trick him. They had thrown every insult and every threat at him, but Jesus never backed down and his answers always left them speechless. Now his popularity had skyrocketed, and the religious leaders wanted him gone.

Caiaphas called the meeting to order and they began to discuss how they could capture Jesus in secret and put him to death.

"But not during the Passover celebration," they agreed, "or the people may riot."

There was a sudden knock at the door, and Judas Iscariot slunk into the room. Satan had entered into him and he had come to speak with the leading priests. He spoke in a low, gravelly voice, "How much will you pay me to betray Jesus to you?"

A surprised murmur travelled around the room. None of the men had expected Jesus' own disciple to turn on him. Caiaphas' face lit up with glee as thirty pieces of silver were counted out and handed to Judas.

From that moment on, Judas began to look for his opportunity to betray Jesus.

139.

The Last Supper 1: Jesus Washes His Disciples' Feet

Matthew 26:17-19, Mark 14:12-17, Luke 22:7-14, John 13:1-17

The streets of Jerusalem were buzzing with activity. It was the first day of the Festival of Unleavened Bread, the day when the Passover lambs would be sacrificed and the Passover meal would be eaten.

Over in Bethany, Jesus took Peter and John aside and asked them to go and prepare the Passover meal. "Where do you want us to prepare it?" they asked him.

Jesus told them, "As soon as you enter Jerusalem, a man carrying a pitcher of water will meet you. Follow him. At the house he enters, say to the owner, 'The Teacher asks: Where is the guest room where I can eat the Passover meal with my disciples?' He will take you upstairs to a large room that is already set up. That is where you should prepare our meal."

So Peter and John went down to the city. Just as Jesus had said, a man carrying a large jar of water led them to a house and they were able to prepare the Passover meal there.

Hours later, Jesus and the other disciples arrived. They began to take their places at the table, but Jesus didn't sit down. The disciples watched curiously as he took off his outer robe and wrapped a towel around his waist. Then he filled a large basin with water. Alarm spread across their faces as Jesus knelt before them and began to wash their feet, one by one. The disciples were horrified. Jesus was a rabbi, a respected teacher. He had been exalted by the crowds, and now he was acting as the lowliest servant. Washing dirty feet was such a humiliating task that not even Jewish slaves could be forced to do it!

When it was his turn, Simon Peter pulled his feet away awkwardly. He could not comprehend why Jesus, the King of kings, the Messiah, would want to wash his feet. Peter blinked, not knowing what to do. He had heard Jesus say over and over that whoever wanted to be great in God's Kingdom had to be a servant. That the least would be the greatest and the greatest would become the least. But still he shook his head furiously and exclaimed, "Lord, are you going to wash my feet?"

Jesus smiled at Peter and replied, "You don't understand now what I am doing, but someday you will."

"No," Peter protested, "you will never ever wash my feet!"

But Jesus told him, "Unless I wash you, you won't belong to me."

Peter's mouth hung open in despair. "Then wash my hands and head as well, Lord, not just my feet!"

When Jesus had washed Peter's feet, he patted them dry with the towel around his waist and told his disciples, "A person who has bathed all over does not need to wash, except for the feet, to be entirely clean. And you disciples are clean, but not all of you."

Jesus was talking about Judas, because it was almost time for Judas to betray him. Jesus put his robe back on and sat down. "Do you understand what I was doing? You call me 'Teacher' and 'Lord,' and you are right, because that's what I am. And since I, your Lord and Teacher, have washed your feet, you ought to wash each other's feet. I have given you an example to follow. Do as I have done to you. I tell you the truth, slaves are not greater than their master. Nor is the messenger more important than the one who sends the message. Now that you know these things, God will bless you for doing them."

140.

The Last Supper II: This is My Body, This is My Blood

Matthew 26:26-29,
Mark 14:22-25, Luke 22:15-20

As they reclined at the table, Jesus' eyes rested on each of the men he had shared his heart and soul with. "I have been very eager to eat this Passover meal with you before my suffering begins. For I tell you now that I won't eat this meal again until its meaning is fulfilled in the Kingdom of God."

Jesus took a loaf of bread and thanked God for it. Then he broke it into pieces and passed it out to the men. "Take this and eat it, for this is my body, which is given for you. Do this in remembrance of me."

As Peter took the bread, he remembered something Jesus had once told the crowd. He had said that he was the living bread that came down from heaven, and the bread was his flesh, offered up so that the world may live. Peter frowned as he chewed. He didn't understand it then and he certainly didn't understand it now.

Next Jesus picked up a cup of wine and thanked God for it. He passed the cup around to his disciples and told them, "Each of you drink from it, for this is my blood, which confirms the covenant between God and his people. It is poured out as a sacrifice to forgive the sins of many. Mark my words - I will not drink wine again until the day I drink it new with you in my Father's Kingdom."

141.

The Last Supper III: Jesus Predicts His Betrayal

Matthew 26:20-25, Mark 14:18-21, Luke 22:21-23, John 13:18-30

As they continued their meal, Jesus was deeply troubled in his spirit. Suddenly he exclaimed, "I tell you the truth, one of you will betray me!"

The men around the table stared at each other in dismay and wondered who Jesus meant. Simon Peter caught John's eye and motioned to him that he should ask Jesus who it was. John hesitated, then he leaned back against Jesus' shoulder and whispered, "Lord, who is it?"

Jesus answered quietly, "It is the one to whom I give the bread I dip in the bowl."

John watched with wide eyes as Jesus dipped the bread. He held his breath as Jesus stretched out his arm and hoped with all his heart that it wouldn't be his brother, James. Relief flooded through him as Judas Iscariot took the bread from Jesus' fingers and put it in his mouth.

As soon as Judas had eaten the bread, Satan entered into him again and Jesus spoke to him in a low voice, "Hurry and do what you're going to do."

None of the other disciples knew what Jesus meant. They thought Judas was going to go and pay for the food or give some money to the poor, because he was the treasurer. But Judas didn't look back as he left the room and went out into the darkness.

142.

The Last Supper IV: Jesus Predicts Peter's Denial

Matthew 26:31-35, Mark 14:27-31,
Luke 22:31-34, John 13:31-38

As soon as Judas was gone, Jesus said, "The time has come for the Son of Man to enter into his glory, and God will be glorified because of him. And since God receives glory because of the Son, he will give his own glory to the Son, and he will do so at once. Dear children, I will be with you only a little longer. And as I told the Jewish leaders, you will search for me, but you can't come where I am going. So now I am giving you a new commandment: Love each other. Just as I have loved you, you should love each other. Your love for one another will prove to the world that you are my disciples."

Simon Peter asked, "Lord, where are you going?"

Jesus replied, "You can't go with me now, but you will follow me later."

Peter frowned, "But why can't I come now, Lord? I'm ready to die for you."

Jesus looked Peter in the eyes. "Simon, Simon, Satan has asked to sift each of you like wheat. But I have pleaded in prayer for you, Simon, that your faith should not fail. So when you have repented and turned to me again, strengthen your brothers."

He held Peter's gaze and when he spoke again, his voice trembled. "Tonight all of you will desert me. For the Scriptures say,

'God will strike the Shepherd,
   and the sheep of the flock will be scattered.'

But after I have been raised from the dead, I will go ahead of you to Galilee and meet you there."

Peter was shocked. He leaned forward and declared, "Even if everyone else deserts you, I will never desert you."

Jesus smiled sadly. "I tell you the truth, Peter - this very night, before the rooster crows, you will deny three times that you even know me."

Peter blinked. "No!" he insisted, emotion rising in his voice. "Even if I have to die with you, I will never deny you!"

The other disciples vowed the same. As Peter sank back, a heavy feeling of despair settled in his chest. His eyes met John's and they stared at each other in bewilderment.

143.

The Last Supper V: The Way to the Father

Luke 22:35-38, John 14:1-14

The disciples ate in silence, each man lost in his own thoughts. Jesus asked them, "When I sent you out to preach the Good News and you did not have money, a traveller's bag, or an extra pair of sandals, did you need anything?"

"No," they answered.

"But now take your money and a traveller's bag. And if you don't have a sword, sell your cloak and buy one! For the time has come for this prophecy about me to be fulfilled: 'He was counted among the rebels.' Yes, everything written about me by the prophets will come true."

The disciples frowned. "Look, Lord, we have two swords among us."

Jesus nodded, "That's enough."

He studied his men. In a few hours their world would be turned upside down and their hearts would be shattered. Jesus smiled grimly. "Don't let your hearts be troubled. Trust in God, and trust also in me. There is more than enough room in my Father's home. If this were not so, would I have told you that I am going to prepare a place for you? When everything is ready, I will come and get you, so that you will always be with me where I am. And you know the way to where I am going."

Thomas was perplexed. "No, we don't know, Lord. We have no idea where you are going, so how can we know the way?"

Jesus answered, "I am the way, the truth, and the life. No one can come to the Father except through me. If you had really known me, you would know who my Father is. From now on, you do know him and have seen him!"

Philip leaned towards Jesus and said, "Lord, show us the Father, and we will be satisfied."

Jesus sighed, "Have I been with you all this time, Philip, and yet you still don't know who I am? Anyone who has seen me has seen the Father! So why are you asking me to show him to you? Don't you believe that I am in the Father and the Father is in me? The words I speak are not my own, but my Father who lives in me does his work through me. Just believe that I am in the Father and the Father is in me. Or at least believe because of the work you have seen me do."

Jesus paused. "I tell you the truth, anyone who believes in me will do the same works I have done, and even greater works, because I am going to be with the Father. You can ask for anything in my name, and I will do it, so that the Son can bring glory to the Father. Yes, ask me for anything in my name, and I will do it!"

144.

The Last Supper VI: Jesus Promises the Holy Spirit

John 14:15-31

"If you love me, obey my commandments. And I will ask the Father, and he will give you another Advocate, who will never leave you. He is the Holy Spirit, who leads into all truth. The world cannot receive him, because it isn't looking for him and doesn't recognise him. But you know him, because he lives with you now and later will be in you."

Jesus' heart ached with love for the eleven men surrounding him. They didn't understand his words now, but one day they would.

"No, I will not abandon you as orphans - I will come to you. Soon the world will no longer see me, but you will see me. Since I live, you also will live. When I am raised to life again, you will know that I am in my Father, and you are in me, and I am in you. Those who accept my commandments and obey them are the ones who love me. And because they love me, my Father will love them. And I will love them and reveal myself to each of them."

Thaddaeus spoke up. "Lord, why are you going to reveal yourself only to us and not to the world at large?"

Jesus told him, "All who love me will do what I say. My Father will love them, and we will come and make our home with each of them. Anyone who doesn't love me will not obey me. And remember, my words are not my own. What I am telling you is from the Father who sent me. I am telling you these things now while I am still with you. But when the Father sends the Advocate as my representative - that is, the Holy Spirit - he will teach you everything and will remind you of everything I have told you.

"I am leaving you with a gift - peace of mind and heart. And the peace I give is a gift the world cannot give. So don't be troubled or afraid. Remember what I told you: I am going away, but I will come back to you again. If you really loved me, you would be happy that I am going to the Father, who is greater than I am. I have told you these things before they happen so that when they do happen, you will believe.

"I don't have much more time to talk to you, because the ruler of this world approaches. He has no power over me, but I will do what the Father requires of me, so that the world will know that I love the Father."

145.

The Last Supper VII: The Greatest Love and The World's Hatred

John 15

Jesus was running out of time. He told his disciples, "I am the true grapevine, and my Father is the gardener. He cuts off every branch of mine that doesn't produce fruit, and he prunes the branches that do bear fruit so they will produce even more. You have already been pruned and purified by the message I have given you. Remain in me, and I will remain in you. For a branch cannot produce fruit if it is severed from the vine, and you cannot be fruitful unless you remain in me.

"Yes, I am the vine; you are the branches. Those who remain in me, and I in them, will produce much fruit. For apart from me you can do nothing.

Anyone who does not remain in me is thrown away like a useless branch and withers. Such branches are gathered into a pile to be burned. But if you remain in me and my words remain in you, you may ask for anything you want, and it will be granted! When you produce much fruit, you are my true disciples. This brings great glory to my Father.

"I have loved you even as the Father has loved me. Remain in my love. When you obey my commandments, you remain in my love, just as I obey my Father's commandments and remain in his love. I have told you these things so that you will be filled with my joy. Yes, your joy will overflow! This is my commandment: Love each other in the same way I have loved you. There is no greater love than to lay down one's life for one's friends. You are my friends if you do what I command. I no longer call you slaves, because a master doesn't confide in his slaves. Now you are my friends, since I have told you everything the Father told me. You didn't choose me. I chose you. I appointed you to go and produce lasting fruit, so that the Father will give you whatever you ask for, using my name. This is my command: Love each other."

Jesus looked intently at his disciples. From Simon Peter, the impulsive fisherman, to Matthew, the dishonest tax collector. They were unlikely friends before they met him, but now they had become brothers, united by the grace of Jesus.

Jesus told them, "If the world hates you, remember that it hated me first. The world would love you as one of its own if you belonged to it, but you are no longer part of the world. I chose you to come out of the world, so it hates you. Do you remember what I told you? 'A slave is not greater than the master.' Since they persecuted me, naturally they will persecute you. And if they had listened to me, they would listen to you. They will do all this to you because of me, for they have rejected the one who sent me. They would not be guilty if I had not come and spoken to them. But now they have no excuse for their sin. Anyone who hates me also hates my Father. If I hadn't done such miraculous signs among them that no one else could do, they would not be guilty. But as it is, they have seen everything

I did, yet they still hate me and my Father. This fulfills what is written in their Scriptures: 'They hated me without cause.'

"But I will send you the Advocate - the Spirit of truth. He will come to you from the Father and will testify all about me. And you must also testify about me because you have been with me from the beginning of my ministry."

146.
The Last Supper VIII: Sadness Will Be Turned to Joy

John 16

"I have told you these things so that you won't abandon your faith. For you will be expelled from the synagogues, and the time is coming when those who kill you will think they are doing a holy service for God. This is because they have never known the Father or me. Yes, I'm telling you these things now, so that when they happen, you will remember my warning. I didn't tell you earlier because I was going to be with you for a while longer.

"But now I am going away to the one who sent me, and not one of you is asking where I am going. Instead, you grieve because of what I've told you. But in fact, it is best for you that I go away, because if I don't, the

Advocate won't come. If I do go away, then I will send him to you. And when he comes, he will convict the world of its sin, and of God's righteousness, and of the coming judgment. The world's sin is that it refuses to believe in me. Righteousness is available because I go to the Father, and you will see me no more. Judgment will come because the ruler of this world has already been judged.

"There is so much more I want to tell you, but you can't bear it now. When the Spirit of truth comes, he will guide you into all truth. He will not speak on his own but will tell you what he has heard. He will tell you about the future."

Jesus paused again and met his disciples' eyes. "In a little while you won't see me anymore. But a little while after that, you will see me again."

The disciples were baffled, and they asked each other quietly, "What does he mean when he says, 'In a little while you won't see me, but then you will see me,' and 'I am going to the Father'? And what does he mean by 'a little while'? We don't understand."

Jesus watched his men as they struggled to understand what he was saying. He had told them many times that he would be crucified and killed, but it never occurred to them that he meant it literally. A dead Messiah made no sense.

Jesus interrupted them. "Are you asking yourselves what I meant? I said in a little while you won't see me, but a little while after that you will see me again. I tell you the truth, you will weep and mourn over what is going to happen to me, but the world will rejoice. You will grieve, but your grief will suddenly turn to wonderful joy. It will be like a woman suffering the pains of labour. When her child is born, her anguish gives way to joy because she has brought a new baby into the world. So you have sorrow now, but I will see you again; then you will rejoice, and no one can rob you of that joy. At that time you won't need to ask me for anything. I tell you the truth, you will ask the Father directly, and he will grant your request because you use my name. You haven't done this before. Ask, using my name, and you will receive, and you will have abundant joy.

"But the time is coming - indeed it's here now - when you will be scattered, each one going his own way, leaving me alone. Yet I am not alone because the Father is with me. I have told you all this so that you may have peace in me. Here on earth you will have many trials and sorrows. But take heart, because I have overcome the world."

147.

The Last Supper IX: The Prayer of Jesus

John 17

Jesus lifted his eyes to heaven and breathed out slowly. Then he prayed, "Father, the hour has come. Glorify your Son so he can give glory back to you. For you have given him authority over everyone. He gives eternal life to each one you have given him. And this is the way to have eternal life - to know you, the only true God, and Jesus Christ, the one you sent to earth. I brought glory to you here on earth by completing the work you gave me to do. Now, Father, bring me into the glory we shared before the world began.

"I have revealed you to the ones you gave me from this world. They were always yours. You gave them to me, and they have kept your word. Now they know that everything I have is a gift from you, for I have passed on to them the message you gave me. They accepted it and know that I came from you, and they believe you sent me.

"My prayer is not for the world, but for those you have given me, because they belong to you. All who are mine belong to you, and you have given them to me, so they bring me glory. Now I am departing from the world; they are staying in this world, but I am coming to you. Holy Father, you have given me your name; now protect them by the power of your name so that they will be united just as we are. During my time here, I protected them by the power of the name you gave me. I guarded them so that not one was lost, except the one headed for destruction, as the Scriptures foretold.

"Now I am coming to you. I told them many things while I was with them in this world so they would be filled with my joy. I have given them your word. And the world hates them because they do not belong to the world, just as I do not belong to the world. I'm not asking you to take them out of the world, but to keep them safe from the evil one. They do not belong to this world any more than I do. Make them holy by your truth; teach them your word, which is truth. Just as you sent me into the world, I am sending them into the world. And I give myself as a holy sacrifice for them so they can be made holy by your truth.

"I am praying not only for these disciples but also for all who will ever believe in me through their message. I pray that they will all be one, just as you and I are one - as you are in me, Father, and I am in you. And may they be in us so that the world will believe you sent me.

"I have given them the glory you gave me, so they may be one as we are one. I am in them and you are in me. May they experience such perfect unity that the world will know that you sent me and that you love them as much as you love me. Father, I want these whom you have given me to be with me where I am. Then they can see all the glory you gave me because you loved me even before the world began!

"O righteous Father, the world doesn't know you, but I do; and these disciples know you sent me. I have revealed you to them, and I will continue to do so. Then your love for me will be in them, and I will be in them."

148.

The Garden of Gethsemane

Matthew 26:36-46,
Mark 14:32-42, Luke 22:39-46

Jesus clenched his jaw and gripped the table with both hands. His stomach was a ball of knots and his heart was overwhelmed with grief. The Passover meal was almost over and he knew it was time to go out and wait for Judas. As he sang the final hymn, the words came from the very depths of his soul.

"The Lord is God, shining upon us.
    Take the sacrifice and bind it with cords on the altar.
You are my God, and I will praise you!

You are my God, and I will exalt you!
Give thanks to the Lord, for he is good!
His faithful love endures forever."

Jesus lead his disciples out of the upper room and across the Kidron Valley towards the Mount of Olives. They came to the garden of Gethsemane, a place they had visited many times before. Jesus told them, "Sit here while I go and pray."

Then he took Peter, James and John with him into the garden. With every step, Jesus grew more and more distressed. His breathing was too fast and uneven, and he groaned in despair, "My soul is crushed with grief to the point of death. Stay here and keep watch with me."

Jesus went further into the garden by himself. His chest heaved with every breath and his heart pounded. The full weight of his mission overcame him and he fell face down on the ground. "Abba, Father!" Jesus' voice cracked in anguish. "Everything is possible for you. Please take this cup of suffering away from me. Yet I want your will to be done, not mine."

Meanwhile, Peter, James and John had tried to stay awake, but their bellies were full and their eyelids were heavy. They woke with a start when Jesus shook Peter. "Simon, are you asleep? Couldn't you watch with me even one hour? Keep watch and pray, so that you will not give in to temptation. For the spirit is willing, but the body is weak."

Jesus left the men and went deeper into the garden again. He fell on his knees and sobbed. "My Father! If this cup cannot be taken away unless I drink it, your will be done."

When he returned to the disciples again, he found them still sleeping. They could not keep their eyes open, and they didn't know what to say to Jesus. So he left them and went back to pray for a third time. By now his spirit was in agony and he groaned in torment. Hot tears ran down his face and beads of sweat fell to the dirt like great drops of blood. Jesus knew he could call on a whole army of angels and they would be at his side in an instant. With one word he could skip the pain, the suffering and the torture that was now only hours away. Jesus broke down and wept.

At last he stood and lifted his tear-stained face to heaven. The whole world was at stake and he would not abandon his mission. He returned to his disciples one last time. "Go ahead and sleep. Have your rest. But no - the time has come. The Son of Man is betrayed into the hands of sinners. Up, let's be going. Look, my betrayer is here!"

The sleepy disciples stood up and followed Jesus through the darkness to meet the man who would betray him.

149.

Jesus is Arrested

Matthew 26:47-56, Mark 14:43-52,
Luke 22:47-53, John 18:2-11

At that moment, Judas entered the garden. A band of soldiers followed closely behind, along with some officers and elders who had been sent by the leading priests and the Pharisees. They carried blazing torches and lanterns, along with swords and clubs.

Judas had already arranged a signal for the soldiers: "You will know which one to arrest when I greet him with a kiss." He walked straight to Jesus and kissed him. "Greetings, Rabbi!"

Jesus looked into Judas' eyes. "Judas, would you betray the Son of Man with a kiss?"

Then Jesus turned and stepped bravely towards the soldiers. "Who are you looking for?"

"Jesus the Nazarene," they replied.

"I am he."

As Jesus said the words, they all drew back and fell onto the ground.

He asked them again, "Who are you looking for?"

The soldiers got to their feet and answered hesitantly, "Jesus the Nazarene."

"I told you that I am he," Jesus said. "And since I am the one you want, let these others go."

As the soldiers grabbed Jesus to arrest him, the disciples began to panic.

"Lord, should we fight? We brought the swords!"

Peter's heart was racing as he drew his sword. He slashed at Malchus, who was a servant of the high priest, and sliced his right ear off. Malchus clutched the side of his head, his eyes wide with shock.

Jesus turned on Peter and reprimanded him sharply, "Put away your sword. Those who use the sword will die by the sword. Don't you realise that I could ask my Father for thousands of angels to protect us, and he would send them instantly? But if I did, how would the Scriptures be fulfilled that describe what must happen now?"

Peter's sword dropped to the ground with a soft thud and he sank to his knees. Jesus reached out his hand and touched Malchus' ear. When he took his hand away, the ear was perfectly whole.

Jesus faced the other officers. "Am I some dangerous revolutionary, that you come with swords and clubs to arrest me? Why didn't you arrest me in the Temple? I was there every day. But this is your moment, the time when the power of darkness reigns."

As they led Jesus away, the terrified disciples deserted him and fled into the night.

150.

Peter's First Denial

John 18:15-18

Simon Peter stayed out of sight as he followed the soldiers through the dark streets of Jerusalem. His heart was thumping so loudly in his chest he was sure they would turn around and see him at any moment. When they came to the home of Caiaphas, Peter stood outside the gates and watched as the soldiers hustled Jesus into the house. The heavy door closed with a final thud behind him.

Another disciple had also followed Jesus. This disciple was known to the high priest and had entered the courtyard without any trouble. When he saw Peter on the other side of the gate, he spoke to the servant girl keeping watch and convinced her to let him in. She studied Peter carefully as he passed through the gate, and asked him, "You're not one of that man's disciples, are you?"

Peter's heart lurched with fear and he stared wide eyed at the girl. "No, I am not."

A group of guards and household servants had lit a charcoal fire in the courtyard to keep warm. Peter hurried away from the girl and stood by the fire, trying desperately to ward off the chill that had settled in his heart.

151.

Jesus Before the High Council

Matthew 26:57-68, Mark 14:53-65,
Luke 22:63-71, John 18:19-24

Inside the house, Jesus was taken to Annas, the father-in-law of Caiaphas. Annas wasted no time and began asking Jesus questions about his disciples and the things he had been teaching them.

Jesus looked him in the eye and answered, "Everyone knows what I teach. I have preached regularly in the synagogues and the Temple, where the people gather. I have not spoken in secret. Why are you asking me this question? Ask those who heard me. They know what I said."

Jesus was thrown backwards as one of the officers hit him across the face with the back of his hand. "Is that the way to answer the high priest?" he growled.

Jesus tasted blood and replied slowly, "If I said anything wrong, you must prove it. But if I'm speaking the truth, why are you beating me?"

Annas scowled. He bound Jesus and sent him to Caiaphas.

Although it was now very late, the teachers of religious law, the elders and the entire high council had gathered. They had been waiting for this moment, and every eye followed Jesus as he entered the room. They finally had him. The men interrogated Jesus relentlessly, desperate to find evidence against him so they could sentence him to death. Many false witnesses came forward and testified, but each time somebody new spoke, he contradicted the person before him. Finally, two men stood up and declared, "This man said, 'I am able to destroy the Temple of God and rebuild it in three days.'"

A cry of outrage exploded across the room and the men hissed at Jesus. Caiaphas shouted for order. Then he stood up and spoke to Jesus in a low, dangerous voice. "Well, aren't you going to answer these charges? What do you have to say for yourself?"

The room was deathly quiet as everybody waited to hear Jesus' response. But he remained silent. Caiaphas grew more furious by the second and he finally exploded, "I demand in the name of the living God - tell us if you are the Messiah, the Son of God."

This was it. Jesus breathed out and calmly replied, "I am. And you will see the Son of Man seated in the place of power at God's right hand and coming on the clouds of heaven."

In that moment, in front of the high priest and the entire high council, Jesus declared himself equal to God. Under Jewish law it was the highest form of heresy, and heresy demanded the death penalty. Every man in the room roared with fury. This was exactly what they had been waiting for! Caiaphas tore his robe in horror and wailed, "Why do we need other witnesses? You have all heard his blasphemy. What is your verdict?"

The men cried out with one voice. "Guilty! He deserves to die!"

Some of the men closest to Jesus began to spit on him. They blindfolded him and hit him in the face with their fists. Then they jeered, "Prophesy to us, you Messiah! Who hit you that time?"

But Jesus said nothing.

152.
Peter's Second and Third Denials

Matthew 26:69-75, Mark 14:66-72,
Luke 22:54-62, John 18:25-27

Meanwhile, back by the fire in the courtyard, Peter stared into the flames. A servant girl had been watching him closely and she said to the people standing nearby, "This man was with Jesus of Nazareth."

Peter looked up quickly and denied Jesus again. "I don't even know the man."

He moved nervously away and stood at the edge of the courtyard. But a short time later, some other bystanders approached him. "You must be one of them; we can tell by your Galilean accent."

Another man, who was a servant of the high priest and a relative of Malchus, whose ear had been cut off, said to Peter, "Didn't I see you out there in the olive grove with Jesus?"

Peter's mouth dropped open and he swore an oath, denying Jesus for the third time. "A curse on me if I'm lying - I don't know the man!"

Across the courtyard, the doors of the house banged open and the guards led Jesus out. At that same moment, the first rooster crowed. Jesus looked back and his eyes locked on Peter's. Peter remembered what Jesus had said and his blood ran cold. "Before the rooster crows, you will deny me three times." A wave of unbearable grief swept over him and he fled from the courtyard, weeping bitterly.

153.

Judas Hangs Himself

Matthew 27:3-10

The first rays of sunlight were beginning to peek over the Judean hills. It was Friday morning, and the members of the high council were still awake, trying to work out how they could convince the Roman governor to kill Jesus. They had condemned him to death, but they still had a problem. They did not have the authority to carry out the death penalty themselves. The Romans had to give them permission to do it.

There was a disturbance at the door and Judas Iscariot burst into the room. When he learned that Jesus had been sentenced to death, he was filled with remorse. He stood in the middle of the high council and cried, "I have sinned! For I have betrayed an innocent man."

Laughter echoed around the room. "What do we care?" the Jewish leaders scoffed. "That's your problem."

Judas groaned in despair and threw the thirty pieces of silver at their feet. He stumbled blindly out into the sunlight, overwhelmed by the terrible thing he had done. Then he went out and hanged himself.

154.

Jesus' Trial Before Pilate

Matthew 27:11-14, Mark 15:1-5,
Luke 23:1-12, John 18:28-38

Pontius Pilate frowned in annoyance. The last thing he wanted this early in the morning was a religious issue to deal with. But Caiaphas and the entire high council had gathered outside his gates and they were getting louder by the minute.

Pilate looked down from his balcony and studied Jesus. He called out to the Jewish leaders, "What is your charge against this man?"

"We wouldn't have handed him over to you if he weren't a criminal!" they replied, avoiding the question. Blasphemy was a Jewish offense and they knew Pilate wouldn't do what they wanted if that was the only charge they had on Jesus.

Pilate scowled, "Then take him away and judge him by your own law."

Pilate couldn't care less about the Jewish religion. His job, as the governor, was only to keep the peace and report to Rome.

But the Jewish leaders would not be put off. "Only the Romans are permitted to execute someone," they called.

Pilate shook his head and went back inside. Then he called for Jesus to be brought to him.

Once they were alone, Pilate asked him, "Are you the king of the Jews?"

Jesus answered, "Is this your own question, or did others tell you about me?"

Pilate snorted. "Am I a Jew? Your own people and their leading priests brought you to me for trial. Why? What have you done?"

Jesus looked Pilate in the eye and answered, "My Kingdom is not an earthly kingdom. If it were, my followers would fight to keep me from being handed over to the Jewish leaders. But my Kingdom is not of this world."

Pilate frowned. "So you are a king?"

"You say I am a king. Actually, I was born and came into the world to testify to the truth. All who love the truth recognise that what I say is true."

Pilate looked out the window and sighed, "What is truth?"

Outside the gates, the religious leaders grew louder and louder as they shouted their accusations against Jesus.

Pilate asked him, "Aren't you going to answer them? What about all these charges they are bringing against you?"

But much to Pilate's surprise, Jesus said nothing. Pilate went outside and yelled, "I find nothing wrong with this man!"

The crowd was growing larger, and the Jewish leaders were becoming more and more desperate. "But he is causing riots by his teaching wherever he goes - all over Judea, from Galilee to Jerusalem!"

When Pilate realised Jesus was Galilean, he was relieved that he might be able to pass on the problem after all. Herod Antipas was the ruler of Galilee and was also visiting Jerusalem for the Passover. His headquarters were not far away, so Pilate sent Jesus to him.

Herod was delighted to see Jesus. He had heard all about him and had been hoping for a long time to see a miracle for himself. He asked question after question, but Jesus would not answer any one of them. Herod finally grew bored, and he and his soldiers began to mock and ridicule Jesus instead. Then they put a royal robe on him and sent him through the streets of Jerusalem, back to Pilate.

155.

Jesus Sentenced to Death

Matthew 27:15-31, Mark 15:6-20,
Luke 23:13-25, John 18:39-19:1-16

Pilate stood Jesus before the crowd to announce his verdict. "You brought this man to me, accusing him of leading a revolt. I have examined him thoroughly on this point in your presence and find him innocent. Herod came to the same conclusion and sent him back to us. Nothing this man has done calls for the death penalty. So I will have him flogged, and then I will release him."

A mighty roar rose from the crowd. They shouted, "Kill him, and release Barabbas to us!"

Every year during the Passover, the governor would release one prisoner. The people could choose anyone they wanted. Barabbas was a violent criminal who had been convicted of murder and insurrection against the government. Pilate tried to argue with the crowd because he wanted to release Jesus. "Would you like me to release to you this 'King of the Jews'?"

But the crowd shouted even louder, "No! Not this man. We want Barabbas!"

Just then Pilate received a message from his wife. "Leave that innocent man alone. I suffered through a terrible nightmare about him last night."

Pilate glanced uneasily at Jesus, while the crowd below chanted louder and louder, "Barabbas! Barabbas! Barabbas! Barabbas!"

Pilate shook his head and asked one more time, "Which of these two do you want me to release to you?"

Their reply was deafening, "BARABBAS!"

Pilate knew he wasn't going to change their minds, and they were close to starting a riot. So he gave the order and Barabbas was released. Pilate asked the crowd, "Then what should I do with Jesus who is called the Messiah?"

"Crucify him!" they shouted back.

"Why?" Pilate demanded. "What crime has he committed? I have found no reason to sentence him to death. So I will have him flogged, and then I will release him."

Pilate handed Jesus over to the soldiers and they took him out to their barracks. They stripped him and tied his hands to a post. They flogged him with a lead tipped whip, over and over, until he was unrecognisable. They twisted together a crown of thorns and laughed as they pushed the long, sharp spikes into his head. Then they put the purple robe back on his body and put a stick in his hand as a scepter. The soldiers knelt before Jesus, pretending to worship him. They laughed, "Hail! King of the Jews!" Then they spat on him, slapped him in the face and beat him with the stick.

When the cruel soldiers had finally had enough, they took Jesus back to Pilate. Pilate went out to address the crowd. "I am going to bring him out to you now, but understand clearly that I find him not guilty."

Jesus stumbled out wearing the blood-stained robe over his shoulders and the crown of thorns on his head. He struggled to stand and pain ripped through his body when he moved. The roar of the crowd filled his ears. "Crucify him! Crucify him!"

"Take him yourselves and crucify him," Pilate said in disgust. "I find him not guilty."

The Jewish leaders replied, "By our law he ought to die because he called himself the Son of God."

When Pilate heard this, he was more afraid than ever. He took Jesus back inside and asked him, "Where are you from?"

But Jesus said nothing.

"Why don't you talk to me?" Pilate demanded. "Don't you realise that I have the power to release you or crucify you?"

Jesus glanced at Pilate through swollen eyes, and answered, "You would have no power over me at all unless it were given to you from above. So the one who handed me over to you has the greater sin."

Pilate stared at Jesus for a long time. Then he went out and tried to release him once more. But the Jewish leaders told him, "If you release this man, you are no 'friend of Caesar.' Anyone who declares himself a king is a rebel against Caesar."

Pilate realised they had him trapped. When Jesus called himself the Son of God, it was blasphemy to the Jews and Pilate didn't care. But anybody who called themselves a king was committing a capital crime against Rome. Pilate's hands were finally tied.

He brought Jesus out one last time. Then he sat in the judgment seat on the platform and said to the people, "Look, here is your king!"

"Away with him!" the people cried angrily. "Away with him! Crucify him!"

"What? Crucify your king?" Pilate asked.

"We have no king but Caesar," the leading priests shouted back.

Pilate shook his head at the irony of their words. They were so desperate to be rid of Jesus they would even declare loyalty to Caesar over their God. Pilate sent for a basin of water, then he washed his hands before the people. "I am innocent of this man's blood. The responsibility is yours!"

They shouted back wildly, "We will take responsibility for his death - we and our children!"

So Pilate handed Jesus over to the Roman soldiers to be put to death by crucifixion, the harshest and most barbaric penalty permitted under Roman law. The soldiers put Jesus' own clothes back on him and led him away.

156.

The Crucifixion

Matthew 27:32-44, Mark 15:21-32,
Luke 23:26-43, John 19:17-24

Every step was unbearable. His tunic stuck to the blood on his back and pain seared through his wounds. The weight of the heavy crossbeam was torturous as it pressed down on his lacerated shoulders. Jesus stumbled and fell heavily to the ground, but the soldiers dragged him roughly back to his feet. He took two more agonising steps and collapsed once more.

A man from Cyrene, named Simon, was coming into the city from the countryside. He was startled when a soldier suddenly grabbed him and ordered him to pick up the crossbeam that Jesus could no longer carry. Simon looked down at Jesus, and wondered what on earth this man had done to deserve such an horrific death.

A large crowd of people followed behind as they moved slowly along the road. Many of them taunted Jesus and called out insults. Others grieved. Jesus turned to a group of women whose faces were wet with tears. He told them through gritted teeth, "Daughters of Jerusalem, don't weep for me, but weep for yourselves and for your children. For if these things are done when the tree is green, what will happen when it is dry?"

When they finally came to Golgotha, also known as 'The Place of the Skull' or Calvary, they offered Jesus some wine mixed with myrrh to dull the pain, but he refused to drink it.

Then they crucified him.

The soldiers stretched his arms out along the crossbeam and drove great long nails through his hands into the wood. Then they drove one long nail through both of his feet. Jesus' eyes rolled back in agony as his cross was hoisted upright and set in place.

Two criminals were crucified with Jesus. One on his left and one on his right. Pilate posted a sign above Jesus' head that read, "JESUS OF NAZARETH, THE KING OF THE JEWS." It was written in Aramaic, in Latin, and in Greek so that many people could read it. When the leading priests saw the sign, they objected and said to Pilate, "Change it from 'The King of the Jews' to 'He said, I am King of the Jews.'"

Pilate shrugged and replied, "No, what I have written, I have written."

Below Jesus, the Roman soldiers made crude jokes and laughed sadistically. The religious leaders sneered in hateful triumph. The people in the crowd watched on in amusement.

Jesus turned his face to heaven and gasped, "Father, forgive them, for they don't know what they are doing."

While Jesus hung on the cross, the soldiers divided his clothes between them. His tunic was seamless, woven from top to bottom in one piece. Instead of ripping it up, the soldiers cast lots to see who would get to keep it.

This fulfilled the Scripture that says, "They divided my garments among themselves and threw dice for my clothing."

The people in the crowd began to mock and ridicule Jesus. "Look at you now!" they yelled at him. "You said you were going to destroy the Temple and rebuild it in three days. Well then, if you are the Son of God, save yourself and come down from the cross!"

The leading priests and the teachers of religious law joined in. "He saved others," they scoffed, "but he can't save himself! So he is the King of Israel, is he? Let him come down from the cross right now, and we will believe in him! He trusted God, so let God rescue him now if he wants him! For he said, 'I am the Son of God.'"

The crowd laughed.

One of the criminals hanging on the cross beside Jesus taunted him. "So you're the Messiah, are you? Prove it by saving yourself - and us, too, while you're at it!"

But the criminal on the other side rebuked him. "Don't you fear God even when you have been sentenced to die? We deserve to die for our crimes, but this man hasn't done anything wrong."

He looked into Jesus' eyes. "Jesus, remember me when you come into your Kingdom."

Jesus answered him, "I assure you, today you will be with me in paradise."

157.

The Death of Jesus

Matthew 27:45-56, Mark 15:33-41,
Luke 23:44-49, John 19:25-30

Jesus' mother, Mary, wept quietly at the foot of the blood stained cross. Her heart was broken into a thousand pieces and she held Jesus' feet in her hands, kissing them again and again. Simeon's words came back to her with startling clarity. "A sword will pierce your very soul."

John stood nearby, tears streaming down his cheeks as he stared at Jesus. His heart thumped violently inside his chest and every part of his body ached with sorrow. Jesus gazed down at the disciple he loved so dearly.

Through sharp ragged breaths, he said to Mary, "Dear woman, here is your son."

Then he looked at John and gasped, "Here is your mother."

Mary collapsed into John's arms, and he vowed he would take care of her.

At twelve noon, the sun failed and a sudden darkness spread over the land. For three hours it was as dark as midnight, and for the first time in his life, Jesus was abandoned and alone. He looked around wildly and his soul was crushed with fear. At that moment the wrath of God was poured out on him. The punishment for the world's sin was laid upon his shoulders. Jesus was broken.

Finally, at three o'clock he cried out in utter despair, "Eloi, Eloi, lema sabachthani?" which means "My God, my God, why have you abandoned me?"

Some people who were standing nearby misunderstood Jesus and thought he was calling for the prophet Elijah. One of them ran to soak a sponge in sour wine. He put it on a hyssop branch and held it up to Jesus' lips so he could drink. The others said, "Wait! Let's see whether Elijah comes to save him."

Jesus bowed his head and uttered, "It is finished."

Then he gave up his spirit and died.

At that moment the earth shook. Rocks split apart, and tombs opened. In the Temple, the curtain that separated the Most Holy Place was torn in two, from top to bottom. No longer would God dwell there. No longer would the high priest be needed to intercede for the people. No longer would sacrifices be required. Jesus had become the unblemished Passover lamb, the perfect blood sacrifice to atone for sin once and for all. It was done, forever.

A Roman centurion had been keeping watch over Jesus. When he felt the earthquake and saw everything else that took place, he was filled with awe. He stared at Jesus' body and got on his knees. "This man truly was the Son of God!"

158.

The Sin-Bearing Messiah

Isaiah 53

Written between 701 and 681 B.C

   Who has believed our message?
   To whom has the Lord revealed his powerful arm?
My servant grew up in the Lord's presence like a tender green shoot,
   like a root in dry ground.
There was nothing beautiful or majestic about his appearance,
   nothing to attract us to him.
He was despised and rejected -
   a man of sorrows, acquainted with deepest grief.
We turned our backs on him and looked the other way.
   He was despised, and we did not care.
Yet it was our weaknesses he carried;
   it was our sorrows that weighed him down.
And we thought his troubles were a punishment from God,
   a punishment for his own sins!
But he was pierced for our rebellion,
   crushed for our sins.

He was beaten so we could be whole.
   He was whipped so we could be healed.
All of us, like sheep, have strayed away.
   We have left God's paths to follow our own.
Yet the Lord laid on him
   the sins of us all.
He was oppressed and treated harshly,
   yet he never said a word.
He was led like a lamb to the slaughter.
   And as a sheep is silent before the shearers,
   he did not open his mouth.
Unjustly condemned,
   he was led away.
No one cared that he died without descendants,
   that his life was cut short in midstream.
But he was struck down
   for the rebellion of my people.
He had done no wrong
   and had never deceived anyone.
But he was buried like a criminal;
   he was put in a rich man's grave.
But it was the Lord's good plan to crush him
   and cause him grief.
Yet when his life is made an offering for sin,
   he will have many descendants.
He will enjoy a long life,
   and the Lord's good plan will prosper in his hands.
When he sees all that is accomplished by his anguish,
   he will be satisfied.
And because of his experience,
   my righteous servant will make it possible
for many to be counted righteous,
   for he will bear all their sins.

I will give him the honours of a victorious soldier,
    because he exposed himself to death.
He was counted among the rebels.
    He bore the sins of many and interceded for rebels.

159.

The Burial of Jesus

Matthew 27:57-66, Mark 15:42-47,
Luke 23:50-56, John 19:31-42

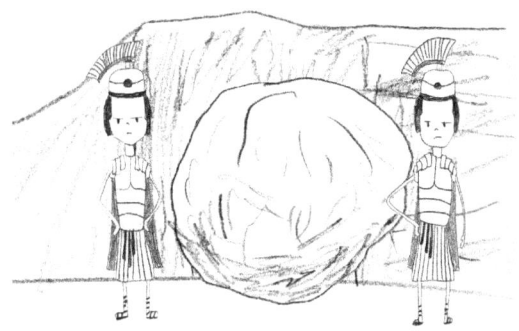

Late in the afternoon, the Jewish leaders approached Pilate. They asked him to break the legs of the crucified men to speed up their deaths. The Sabbath would begin at sundown and they wanted the bodies off the crosses before then. Pilate agreed and gave the order. The two criminals hanging either side of Jesus groaned in agony. But when the soldiers came to Jesus, they didn't break his legs because they realised he was already dead. Instead, one of the soldiers thrust his spear into Jesus' side, causing blood and water to come gushing out. These things fulfilled the Scriptures that said, "Not one of his bones will be broken," and "They will look on the one they pierced."

As evening approached, a rich man from Arimathea, named Joseph, gathered his courage and went to ask Pilate if he could take Jesus' body. Joseph was a prominent member of the high council, but he had not agreed with their decision to crucify Jesus. He was, in fact, a secret follower.

Pilate was surprised and couldn't believe Jesus was already dead. He sent for the centurion to ask if it were true, then he gave Joseph permission to take the body.

Nicodemus went with Joseph, and together they lifted Jesus' body down from the cross and wrapped it in a long sheet of linen cloth. It was getting late and the Sabbath was about to begin. Joseph had his own tomb carved out of rock in a garden nearby, so they laid Jesus' body in there. Then they heaved and pushed a great big stone across the entrance.

A woman named Mary Magdalene had followed with some of the other women from Galilee. Through eyes full of tears, they watched where Jesus was laid. Then they went home and prepared the spices and ointments to anoint his body for burial. By the time they had finished, the Sabbath had begun, and the law required them to stop and rest. They would have to wait until the Sabbath was over before they could anoint Jesus' body.

On Saturday (which was the Sabbath), some of the leading priests and Pharisees went to see Pilate. "Sir, we remember what that deceiver once said while he was still alive: 'After three days I will rise from the dead.' So we request that you seal the tomb until the third day. This will prevent his disciples from coming and stealing his body and then telling everyone he was raised from the dead! If that happens, we'll be worse off than we were at first."

Pilate agreed with the men. "Take guards and secure it the best you can."

So Jesus' tomb was sealed and guards were posted to watch over it.

160.

The Resurrection

Matthew 28:1-10, Mark 16:1-11,
Luke 24:1-12, John 20:1-18

The women hurried anxiously along the road in the semi-darkness, clutching their ointments and burial spices. It was Sunday morning, and they had left the house at the first sign of dawn. Mary Magdalene was among the women, as well as Salome, the mother of James and John. A woman named Joanna and another Mary were also with them. As they came closer to the garden, they asked one another, "Who will roll away the stone for us from the entrance to the tomb?"

But as they came into the garden and saw the tomb, they stopped and stared in surprise. The stone had already been rolled away and an angel of the Lord sat upon it. His face shone like lightning and his clothes were as white as snow. The guards were lying on the ground nearby, because they had fainted in terror. The angel suddenly spoke, and the women fell to their knees, clinging to one another, their eyes wide with fear.

"Don't be afraid!" he said. "Why are you looking among the dead for someone who is alive? He isn't here! He is risen from the dead! Remember what he told you back in Galilee, that the Son of Man must be betrayed into the hands of sinful men and be crucified, and that he would rise again on the third day."

The women were amazed, and their hearts surged with hope. Jesus was alive! They stood up and rushed from the garden, eager to tell the disciples the good news. On the way, Jesus suddenly appeared and greeted them. The women were stunned, and they stared at him in awe. Then they ran to him and began to worship him.

Jesus told them, "Don't be afraid! Go tell my brothers to leave for Galilee, and they will see me there."

Meanwhile in the upper room, the disciples sat in silent darkness. They were terrified of the Jewish leaders and lost in their grief. None of them had any idea what to do next. When Jesus had died, they had all gathered back there and locked the doors. Simon Peter had found the darkest corner to hide in. He had not been able to eat or speak, and his entire body ached with sorrow.

Loud banging on the door made everyone in the room jump, and their eyes opened wide with fear. Somebody unlocked it and the women burst in, their faces glowing with joy. Mary Magdalene stood in the middle of the room and declared breathlessly, "I have seen the Lord!"

Peter leaned forward and listened as the women relayed the whole story about the empty tomb and the angel. Their story sounded like made up nonsense and most of the disciples did not believe them. But Peter and John stared at each other across the room. Then in one swift movement, they were both up and running for the door. John got to the tomb first. He stooped in the doorway and saw the strips of linen. The cloth that had covered Jesus' head was folded up, lying to one side. Peter pushed past John, and his arms hung limply by his sides while his eyes adjusted to the light.

As Peter and John stood side by side in the empty tomb, they saw and they believed. They still did not understand the Scriptures about Jesus having to rise from the dead, but they returned to the upper room filled with wonder and awe.

161.

The Cover Up

Matthew 28:11-15

Across the city, the guards were still weak at the knees as they reported to the leading priests and told them about the angel and the open tomb. The priests gritted their teeth and knew they had a serious problem. How could a body go missing from a tomb that had been sealed and heavily guarded? If the news got out, it would be catastrophic for them.

They immediately called an emergency meeting with the elders, and after much discussion, they formulated a plan to cover up the missing body. They called the guards back in and gave them a large amount of money. Then they instructed them: "You must say, 'Jesus' disciples came during the night while we were sleeping, and they stole his body.' If the governor hears about it, we'll stand up for you so you won't get in trouble."

The guards knew they could be put to death for failing their duties, so they gladly accepted the bribe and said what they were told to say. Their story spread far and wide among the Jews, even to this day.

162.

The Road to Emmaus

Mark 16:12-13, Luke 24:13-34

Later that day, two men were on their way to the village of Emmaus, about eleven kilometres from Jerusalem. As they walked along the road, Jesus himself began walking with them, but God kept them from recognising him.

Jesus asked them, "What are you discussing so intently as you walk along?"

The men stopped and looked at Jesus with eyes full of sorrow. Then one of them, whose name was Cleopas, replied sadly, "You must be the only person in Jerusalem who hasn't heard about all the things that have happened there the last few days."

"What things?" Jesus asked.

"The things that happened to Jesus, the man from Nazareth," they said. "He was a prophet who did powerful miracles, and he was a mighty teacher in the eyes of God and all the people. But our leading priests and other religious leaders handed him over to be condemned to death, and they crucified him. We had hoped he was the Messiah who had come to rescue Israel. This all happened three days ago.

"Then some women from our group of his followers were at his tomb early this morning, and they came back with an amazing report. They said his body was missing, and they had seen angels who told them Jesus is alive! Some of our men ran out to see, and sure enough, his body was gone, just as the women had said."

Jesus sighed, "You foolish people! You find it so hard to believe all that the prophets wrote in the Scriptures. Wasn't it clearly predicted that the Messiah would have to suffer all these things before entering his glory?"

Then Jesus began explaining the Scriptures, beginning with Moses and going through all of the prophets. He interpreted everything that was prophesied about himself, from his birth, to his betrayal, to the exact details of his death.

When they reached the village, Jesus kept walking as though he was going further. But it was getting late, and when the two men begged him to stay, Jesus agreed and went home with them. They sat down to eat, and Jesus took the bread in his hands. He thanked God for it, then broke it and passed it to the men. At that moment their eyes were suddenly opened and they recognised him. Their mouths dropped open and Jesus disappeared.

The men stared at each other in astonishment. "Didn't our hearts burn within us as he talked with us on the road and explained the Scriptures to us?"

They left the bread on the table and hurried all the way back to Jerusalem.

163.

Jesus Appears to his Disciples

Mark 16:14, Luke 24:35-49, John 20:19-23

Back in the upper room, the disciples were still hiding and the doors were still locked. A large group of believers had gathered there with them and they all spoke in low voices, wondering what the empty tomb meant, and what was going to happen next.

Suddenly there was a frantic knock at the door and the two men from Emmaus burst in. The disciples listened in amazement as the men told them how they met Jesus on the road and how they only recognised him after he broke the bread. They were still speaking when Jesus suddenly appeared in the room with them. "Peace be with you."

Every person in the room was terrified, and thought they were looking at a ghost.

"Why are you frightened?" he asked, with a familiar twinkle in his eye. "Why are your hearts filled with doubt? Look at my hands. Look at my feet. You can see that it's really me. Touch me and make sure that I am not a ghost, because ghosts don't have bodies, as you see that I do."

Jesus held out his nail pierced hands and showed them his feet. They all stared in disbelief, but their hearts were filled with wonder and joy.

Jesus looked around and asked, "Do you have anything here to eat?"

Somebody passed him a piece of broiled fish, and they watched in silence as he ate it. Then he said to them, "When I was with you before, I told you that everything written about me in the law of Moses and the prophets and in the Psalms must be fulfilled."

The disciple's minds were suddenly opened so they could understand the Scriptures, and they stared at Jesus in awe as he continued, "Yes, it was written long ago that the Messiah would suffer and die and rise from the dead on the third day. It was also written that this message would be proclaimed in the authority of his name to all the nations, beginning in Jerusalem: 'There is forgiveness of sins for all who repent.' You are witnesses of all these things."

164.

Doubting Thomas

John 20:24-31

Thomas had been out and had missed Jesus' appearance. But when he returned to the upper room, he stared hard at his friends' faces. The fear that had lingered in their eyes was gone. Everything about them was different. Their faces lit up when they saw him, and they all began talking at once. "We have seen the Lord!"

They told Thomas everything that had happened, and all the things Jesus had said. But Thomas was unconvinced. "I won't believe it unless I see the nail wounds in his hands, put my fingers into them, and place my hand into the wound in his side."

Eight days passed, and the disciples remained hidden in the upper room. Their fear slowly returned, and the door remained firmly locked. Suddenly Jesus appeared, just like before, and was standing among them. "Peace be with you."

Thomas' mouth fell open when Jesus looked straight at him. "Put your finger here, and look at my hands. Put your hand into the wound in my side. Don't be faithless any longer. Believe!"

Thomas ran his fingers clumsily over Jesus' hands. Then he touched his side and exclaimed, "My Lord and my God!"

Jesus told him, "You believe because you have seen me. Blessed are those who believe without seeing me."

165.

Jesus Appears in Galilee

John 21:1-23

The disciples returned to Galilee to wait for Jesus. One night Simon Peter told the others, "I'm going fishing."

James, John, Thomas, Nathanael, and two more disciples went with him. The men stayed out all night but did not catch a thing.

As the day was breaking, and they were coming back in, they noticed a man standing on the shore. They couldn't tell who it was, but he called out to them, "Fellows, have you caught any fish?"

"No," they replied.

The man told them, "Throw out your net on the right-hand side of the boat, and you'll get some!"

The disciples threw the net over the right-hand side of the boat and immediately yelled in surprise. The net was so full of fish that they couldn't pull it in.

John looked at Peter and shouted, "It's the Lord!"

Peter's heart leapt in his chest. He grabbed his tunic that he had taken off for work, and quickly pulled it on. Then he threw himself into the sea and swam ashore. The others followed in the boat, dragging the loaded net behind them.

A charcoal fire was burning on the beach with a few fish laid out on it, and some bread. When the boat landed, Jesus asked the men to bring some of the fish they had just caught. Peter climbed back into the boat and helped haul the net ashore. They counted one hundred and fifty-three large fish and were amazed the net had not torn!

"Now come and have some breakfast!" Jesus said. The disciples couldn't take their eyes off him as he served them bread and fish. None of them had to ask if it was really him, because they knew for sure that it was.

After they had eaten, Jesus took Peter aside. They walked along the rocky shore and Jesus asked him, "Simon son of John, do you love me more than these?"

"Yes, Lord," Peter replied, "you know I love you."

"Then feed my lambs," Jesus told him.

They kept walking and Jesus repeated the question: "Simon son of John, do you love me?"

"Yes, Lord," Peter said, staring at him earnestly, "you know I love you."

"Then take care of my sheep."

They sat down next to the waters edge and Jesus asked for the third time, "Simon son of John, do you love me?"

Peter stared deep into Jesus' eyes, distressed that he would have to ask the question three times. He threw a small stone into the water and watched as the ripples spread out in every direction. His voice trembled with emotion, "Lord, you know everything. You know that I love you."

"Then feed my sheep."

As they walked back to join the other disciples, grace and redemption flooded through Peter. The weight of his guilt was lifted from him, and an unfaltering courage took its place. Unlike Judas, who had chosen to die in his sin and shame, Peter was free. He would become the rock of the church, and would live, and die, to serve his King.

166.

The Great Commission

Matthew 28:16-20, Mark 16:15-20,
Luke 24:50-53, Acts 1:3-11

Forty days after Jesus rose from the dead, he led his disciples back to Bethany. He had appeared to them many times, giving them proof beyond a doubt that he was alive, and he spoke to them in detail about the Kingdom of God. He had accomplished his purpose here on earth and was ready to pass on his mission.

As they stood together on the Mount of Olives, he told his disciples, "Do not leave Jerusalem until the Father sends you the gift he promised, as

I told you before. John baptised with water, but in just a few days you will be baptised with the Holy Spirit."

The men asked him eagerly, "Lord, has the time come for you to free Israel and restore our kingdom?"

But Jesus replied, "The Father alone has the authority to set those dates and times, and they are not for you to know. But you will receive power when the Holy Spirit comes upon you. And you will be my witnesses, telling people about me everywhere - in Jerusalem, throughout Judea, in Samaria, and to the ends of the earth."

Jesus studied his disciples. These eleven men, who had deserted him and cowered in an upper room after his death, would never be the same. They had seen the risen King and their fear had given way to unshakeable courage. They were ready to take the gospel to the world.

Jesus gave them their final instructions. "I have been given all authority in heaven and on earth. Therefore, go and make disciples of all the nations, baptising them in the name of the Father and the Son and the Holy Spirit. Teach these new disciples to obey all the commands I have given you. And be sure of this: I am with you always, even to the end of the age."

Then, lifting his hands to heaven, Jesus blessed them. And before their very eyes, he was taken up into heaven, where he sat down in the place of honour at God's right hand. As the disciples stood there, straining their eyes towards the sky, two men dressed in white robes were suddenly standing among them.

"Men of Galilee," they said, "why are you standing here staring into heaven? Jesus has been taken from you into heaven, but someday he will return from heaven in the same way you saw him go!"

The disciples were full of joy as they returned to Jerusalem, with Jesus' words echoing in their hearts. Simon Peter caught John's eye and the two men nodded to each other, their faces shining. James looked back at his brother and grinned. Finally unafraid, the men made their way to the Temple and continued to praise God there.

EPILOGUE

In the three years he had been with them, Jesus had shown his disciples that nobody who says yes to him can remain the same. He had transformed each of these ordinary men into fearless evangelists. They would boldly take Jesus' message to Jerusalem, across the seas and into the heart of Rome. Ten of them would be martyred, killed for their faith in Jesus Christ. But no power in heaven or on earth could stop their message of salvation from spreading throughout the world.

And that is the good news.

What does the good news mean for you and me? Every one of us is going to stand before God and give an account for our lives. The bad news is we are all sinners and we all fall well short of the glory of God. We all deserve judgment and death. But the good news is that he made a way for everybody to escape his judgment and be with him forever. No matter who you are or what you've done, no matter how good you are at keeping the rules, or how badly you mess them up, God loves you and he wants you in his Kingdom. It is as simple, yet as difficult, as giving up your sin and turning to him.

Some people will tell you there are many ways to get to God. But that's not true. Jesus is the one and only way to God. Other people think you can get there by being good enough. But that's not true either. The only way into the Kingdom of God is to lay down your life and surrender to him. Repent of your sin and believe in the one who satisfied God's anger against you when he died in your place and took your punishment: Jesus, the Messiah, the one and only, Saviour of the World.

APPENDIX

Scriptures used in each chapter.
(New Living Translation)

1. **The Eternal Word** John 1:10-13
2. **Zechariah and the Angel** Luke 1:13b-17, 1:18b, 1:19b-20
3. **Mary and the Angel** Luke 1:28b, 1:30-33, 1:34b, 1:35b-37, 1:38b
4. **Joseph and the Angel** Matt 1:20b-21, 1:23
5. **Mary Visits Elizabeth** Luke 1:42b-45, 1:46-55
6. **The Birth of John the Baptist** Luke 1:60b, 1:61, 1:66b, 1:76b-79
7. **The Birth of Jesus** Luke 2:10b-12, 2:14
8. **The Genealogy of Jesus**
9. **Simeon and Anna** Luke 2:29-32, 2:34-35
10. **The Wise Men Find Jesus** Matt 2:2, 2:4, 2:5b-6, 2:8
11. **Escape to Egypt** Matt 2:13b, 2:20
12. **The Boy at the Temple** Luke 2:48, 2:49
13. **A Voice in the Wilderness** Matt 3:2, 3:7b-12, Luke 3:10b, 3:11, 3:12b, 3:13b, 3:14b, John 1:22, 1:23
14. **Jesus is Baptised** Matt 3:14b, 3:15b, 3:17b, John 1:29b-31
15. **Jesus is Tested** Matt 4:3b, 4:4b, 4:6b, 4:7b, 4:9, 4:10b
16. **The Lamb of God** John 1:29b, 1:32b-34, 1:38b, 1:39a, 1:41b
17. **The First Disciples** Matt 4:17b, 4:19b, Luke 5:4b, 5:5b, 5:8b, John 1:42b
18. **Philip and Nathanael** John 1:43b, 1:45b, 1:46b, 1:47b, 1:48, 1:49b, 1:50b, 1:51b
19. **The Wedding at Cana** John 2:3b, 2:4, 2:5b, 2:7b, 2:8b, 2:10
20. **Jesus Casts Out an Unclean Spirit** Mark 1:24, 1:25b, 1:27b
21. **Jesus Heals Many People**
22. **Jesus Preaches in Galilee** Mark 1:37b, Luke 4:43b

23. **Jesus Rejected at Nazareth** Mark 6:2b, 6:3b, Luke 4:18-19, 4:21b, 4:22b, 4:23b-27
24. **Jesus Heals a Leper** Luke 5:12b, 5:13b, 5:14b
25. **Jesus Heals a Paralysed Man** Luke 5:20b, 5:21b, 5:22b-24
26. **Jesus Calls Matthew** Matt 9:11b, Luke 5:27b, 5:31b-32
27. **A Question About Fasting** Mark 2:19b-20, Luke 5:33b, 5:36b-39
28. **Jesus Clears the Temple** John 2:16b, 2:18b, 2:19b, 2:20b
29. **Jesus and Nicodemus** John 3:2b, 3:3b, 3:4, 3:5-8, 3:9a, 3:10, 3:11-15, 3:16-17, 3:18-21, Numbers 21:8b
30. **John the Baptist Exalts Jesus** John 3:26b, 3:27b-29, 3:30, 3:31-36
31. **Jesus and the Samaritan Woman** John 4:9b, 4:10, 4:11-12, 4:13b-14, 4:15b, 4:16a, 4:17b-18, 4:19b-20, 4:21-24, 4:25b, 4:26b, 4:29, 4:32b, 4:33a, 4:34b-38, 4:42b
32. **Jesus Heals on the Sabbath** Matt 12:2b, 12:3b-8, 12:11b-12, Luke 6:8b, 6:9b
33. **God's Chosen Servant** Matt 12:18-21
34. **The Pool of Bethesda** John 5:6b, 5:7b, 5:8, 5:10b, 5:11b, 5:12a, 5:14b
35. **Jesus Claims to be the Son of God** John 5:17b, 5:19b-30, 5:39-47
36. **The Twelve Apostles**
37. **The Sermon on the Mount: Beatitudes** Matt 5:3-10, Luke 6:22-26
38. **The Sermon on the Mount: Salt and Light** Matt 5:13-16
39. **The Sermon on the Mount: Jesus Fulfills the Law** Matt 5:17-20
40. **The Sermon on the Mount: Anger, Adultery, Divorce and Revenge** Matt 5:21-24, 5:27-30, 5:31-32, 5:38-42
41. **The Sermon on the Mount: Love Your Enemies** Matt 5:43-48
42. **The Sermon on the Mount: Treasures in Heaven** Matt 6:1-4, 6:19-21
43. **The Sermon on the Mount: Prayer** Matt 6:5-15
44. **The Sermon on the Mount: Keep Asking, Seeking, Knocking** Luke 11:5-13
45. **The Sermon on the Mount: Judging Others and Fasting** Matt 6:16-18, 7:1-6

46. **The Sermon on the Mount: The Narrow Gate** Matt 7:13-14
47. **The Sermon on the mount: A Tree and its Fruit** Matt 7:15-20, Luke 6:43-45
48. **The Sermon on the Mount: True Disciples** Matt 7:21-23, 7:24-27, Luke 6:46
49. **The Faith of the Centurion** Matt 8:10b-12, 8:13b, Luke 7:4b-5, 7:6b-8
50. **Jesus Raises a Widow's Son** Luke 7:14b, 7:16b
51. **Messengers from John the Baptist** Matt 11:3, 11:4b-5, 11:6b, 11:7-15, Luke 7:31-35
52. **Judgement on Unbelievers** Matt 11:21, 11:22, 11:23-24, 11:25-27, 11:28-30
53. **Jesus Anointed by a Sinful Woman** Luke 7:39b, 7:41b-42, 7:44b-47, 7:48, 7:49b, 7:50b
54. **Jesus and the Prince of Demons** Matt 12:23b, 12:25b-29, 12:30-33, 12:34-37, Mark 3:22b, 3:23b
55. **The True Family of Jesus** Matt 12:47b, 12:48, 12:49b-50, Mark 3:21b
56. **Parable of the Sower** Matt 13:3b-9, 13:10b, 13:11b-17, 13:19-23
57. **Parable of the Wheat and the Weeds** Matt 13:24-30, 13:36b, 13:37b-43
58. **The Kingdom of Heaven** Matt 13:31-35, 13:44-52, Mark 4:21-34, Luke 13:16-21
59. **Jesus Calms the Storm** Matt 8:25b, 8:26b, Mark 4:39b, 4:41b
60. **Jesus Heals a Man with a Demon** Mark 5:9b, Luke 8:28b, 8:39a
61. **The Bleeding Woman and Jairus' Daughter** Matt 9:24b, Mark 5:28b, 5:34b, 5:41b, Luke 8:45b, 8:46b, 8:49b, 8:50b
62. **The Workers Are Few** Matt 9:37b-38
63. **Jesus Sends Out the Twelve Apostles** Matt 10:5-10, 10:14-33, 10:34, 10:36-40, Luke 12:49-50, 12:52-53
64. **The Death of John the Baptist** Mark 6:22b, 6:23b, 6:24b
65. **Jesus Feeds Five Thousand** Mark 6:35b-36, 6:37b, John 6:5b, 6:7b, 6:9, 6:14b

66. **Jesus Walks on Water** Matt 14:28b, 14:30b, 14:31b, 14:33b, John 6:20b
67. **Many Followers Desert Jesus** John 6:25b, 6:26b-27, 6:28b, 6:29, 6:30b, 6:31, 6:32b-34, 6:35b-36, 6:42b, 6:43b-44, 6:47-51, 6:52b, 6:53b-57, 6:60b, 6:61b-64, 6:67b, 6:68-69
68. **Inner Purity** Matt 15:2, 15:10b-11, 15:12b, 15:13-14, 15:20, Mark 7:6b-8, 7:9b-13, 7:18-19, 7:20b-22
69. **The Faith of a Gentile Woman** Matt 15:22b, 15:23b, 15:24b, 15:25b, 15:26b, Mark 7:28b, 7:29
70. **Jesus Feeds Four Thousand** Matt 15:32b, 15:33b, 15:34b, Mark 7:37b
71. **The Pharisees Demand a Sign** Matt 12:38b, 12:39b-42, 16:2b-3
72. **The Yeast of the Pharisees and Sadducees** Matt 16:6b, Mark 8:17b-19, 18:20-21
73. **Peter's Declaration** Matt 16:15b, 16:16b, 16:17b-18, Luke 9:18b-19
74. **Jesus Predicts His Death** Matt 16:22b, 16:23b, Mark 8:34b-38
75. **The Transfiguration** Matt 17:4b, 17:5b, 17:7b, 17:9b, 17:10b, 17:11-12
76. **Jesus Heals a Boy with a Demon** Mark 9:16b, 9:17b-18, 9:19b, 9:21-22, 9:23, 9:24b, 9:25b, 9:28b, 9:29b
77. **Jesus Predicts His Death Again** Mark 9:31b, Luke 9:44
78. **The Temple Tax** Matt 17:24b, 17:25b, 17:26-27
79. **The Greatest in the Kingdom** Matt 18:3b-4, Mark 9:33b, 9:35b, Luke 9:48b
80. **Using the Name of Jesus** Mark 9:38b, 9:39b-41, 9:42-48
81. **Parable of the Unforgiving Servant** Matt 18:15-17, 18:21b, 18:22, 18:23-35
82. **Marriage and Divorce** Matt 19:3b, 19:4, 19:5-6, 19:7a, 19:8b-9, Mark 10:12
83. **Jesus Blesses the Children** Luke 18:16b-17
84. **The Rich Young Man** Mark 10:17b, 10:18-19, 10:20b, 10:21b, 10:23b, 10:25, 10:26b, 10:27b, 10:28b, 10:29-31
85. **Parable of the Vineyard Workers** Matt 20:1-16

86. **The Festival of Shelters** John 7:3b-4, 7:6b-8, 7:12b, 7:15b, 7:16b-19, 7:20b, 7:21b-24, 7:25b-27, 7:28b-29, 7:31b
87. **The People Are Divided** John 7:33b-34, 7:35b-36, 7:37b-38, 7:45b, 7:46a, 7:47a, 7:48-49, 7:51a, 7:52b
88. **A Woman Caught in Adultery** John 8:4b-5, 8:7b, 8:10b, 8:11b
89. **The People Argue with Jesus** John 8:12b, 8:13b, 8:14b-18, 8:19, 8:21b, 8:22b, 8:23-24, 8:25-26, 8:28b-29, 8:31b-32, 8:33b, 8:34b-38, 8:39b-41, 8:42-43, 8:44-47, 8:48b, 8:49b-51, 8:52b-53, 8:54-56, 8:57b, 8:58
90. **Jesus Heals a Man Born Blind** John 9:2b, 9:3b, 9:8b, 9:9b, 9:10b, 9:11-12a, 9:15b, 9:16b, 9:16c, 9:17b, 9:17c, 9:19b, 9:20b-21, 9:24b, 9:25b, 9:26b, 9:27, 9:28b-29, 9:30b-33, 9:34b
91. **Spiritual Blindness** John 9:35b, 9:36b, 9:37, 9:38a, 9:39, 9:40b, 9:41
92. **The Good Shepherd** John 10:1-5, 10:7b-18, 10:20b, 10:21b
93. **Jesus Claims to be the Son of God Again** John 10:24b, 10:25b-30, 10:32b, 10:33b, 10:34b-38, 10:41b
94. **Parable of the Good Samaritan** Luke 10:25b, 10:26b, 10:27b, 10:28b, 10:29b, 10:30b-36, 10:37b
95. **Mary and Martha** Luke 10:40b, 10:41b-42
96. **A Warning Against Hypocrisy** Matt 23:2-3, 23:5-12, 23:13-15, 23:23-24, 23:26b, 23:27-28, 23:29b-36, Luke 11:39b-40, 11:45b, 11:46b-47a
97. **The Narrow Door** Luke 13:23b, 13:24-30
98. **Jesus Grieves for Jerusalem** Luke 13:31b, 13:32b-33, 13:34-35
99. **A Rebellious Nation** Isaiah 1:10-20
100. **Parable of the Rich Fool** Luke 12:13b, 12:14b, 12:15b, 12:16b-21, 12:22-34
101. **A Call to Repentance** Luke 13:2a, 13:3-5, 13:6b-9
102. **Jesus Heals on the Sabbath** Luke 13:12b, 13:14b, 13:15b-16
103. **Humility** Luke 14:3b, 14:5b, 14:8-11, 14:12b-14
104. **A Samaritan Village Rejects Jesus** Luke 9:54, 9:55b-56

105. **The Cost of Following Jesus** Matt 8:19b, 8:20b, 8:21b, 8:22b, Luke 9:61b, 9:62b, 14:26-27, 14:28-33
106. **Parable of the Lost Sheep and the Lost Coin** Luke 15:4-7, 15:8-10
107. **Parable of the Lost Son** Luke 15:11b-32
108. **Parable of the Dishonest Manager** Luke 16:1b-13, 16:15b
109. **The Rich Man and Lazarus** Luke 16:19b-31
110. **Servanthood** Luke 17:7-10
111. **Jesus Heals Ten Lepers** Luke 17:13b, 17:14b, 17:17b-18, 17:19b
112. **Parable of the Persistent Widow** Luke 18:2b-5, 18:6b-8
113. **Parable of the Pharisee and the Tax Collector** Luke 18:10-14
114. **Jesus Raises Lazarus from the Dead** John 11:3b, 11:4b, 11:8b, 11:9b-10, 11:11b, 11:14b-15, 11:21b-22, 12:23b, 11:24b, 11:25b-26, 11:27b, 11:28b, 11:32b, 11:34a, 11:36b, 11:37b, 11:39a, 11:39c, 11:40b, 11:41b-42, 11:43b, 11:44b
115. **The Plot to Kill Jesus** John 11:47b-48, 11:49b-50, 11:56b
116. **Jesus Predicts His Death a Third Time** Luke 18:31b, Mark 10:33c-34
117. **Greatness is Serving** Mark 10:35b, 10:36b, 10:37b, 10:38b, 10:39a, 10:39c-40, 10:42b-45
118. **Jesus and Zacchaeus** Luke 19:5b, 19:7b, 19:8b, 19:9b-10
119. **Blind Bartimaeus** Mark 10:47b, 10:48b, 10:49c, 10:51a, 10:51c, 10:52b
120. **Parable of the Three Servants** Matt 25:14b-30
121. **The Triumphal Entry** Mark 11:2b-3, 11:5b, Luke 19:34b, 19:39b, 19:40b, John 12:13b, 12:15, 12:19b
122. **Jesus Weeps for Jerusalem** Luke 19:42-44
123. **Jesus Anointed at Bethany** Mark 14:6b-9, John 12:5
124. **Jesus Curses the Fig Tree** Matt 21:19c, 21:20b, 21:21b, Mark 11:23b-25
125. **Jesus Clears the Temple Again** Matt 21:15b, 21:16b, 21:16c, Mark 11:17b
126. **The Authority of Jesus Challenged** Matt 21:23c, 21:24a, 21:25a, 21:25c-26, 21:27c-31a, 21:31c-32

127. **Parable of the Evil Farmers** Matt 21:40, 21:41b, 21:42b, 21:43-44, Mark 12:1b-8
128. **The Wedding Banquet** Matt 22:2, 22:10, 22:11-14, Luke 14:17-24
129. **The Son of Man Must Be Lifted Up** John 12:23b, 12:24-26, 12:27-28a, 12:28b, 12:30b-32, 12:34b, 12:35b-36a
130. **The Unbelief of the People** John 12:38b-40, 12:44b-50
131. **The Leaders Try to Trap Jesus** Matt 22:18b, Mark 12:19-23,12:24b-27, Luke 20:21b-22, 20:24, 20:25
132. **The Greatest Commandment** Mark 12:28c,12:29b-31, 12:32b-33, 12:34b
133. **Whose Son is the Messiah?** Matt 22:42b, 22:43b-45
134. **The Widow's Offering** Mark 12:44, Luke 21:3b
135. **The Coming of the Kingdom** Matthew 24:7b-8, 24:9-14, 24:27-31, 24:40-41, Mark 13:1b, 13:2b, 13:4, 13:32b-37, Luke 12:39-40, 12:41b, 12:42b-48, Luke 17:22b-23, 17:26-34, Luke 21:8b-9, 21:10b
136. **Parable of the Ten Bridesmaids** Matt 25:1-13
137. **The Final Judgment** Matt 25:31-46, 26:2
138. **Judas and the Plot to Kill Jesus** Matt 26:5, 26:15b
139. **The Last Supper I: This is My Body, This is My Blood** John 13:6b, 13:7b, 13:8, 13:9b, 13:10b, 13:12b-17, Luke 22:9, 10b-12
140. **The Last Supper II: Jesus Washes His Disciples' Feet** Matt 26:26c, 26:27b-29, Luke 22:15b-16, 22:19c
141. **The Last Supper III: Jesus Predicts His Betrayal** John13:21b, 13:25b, 13:26b, 13:27c
142. **The Last Supper IV: Jesus Predicts Peter's Denial** Matt 26:31b-32, 26:33b, 26:34b, 26:35b, Luke 22:31-32, John 13:31b-35, 13:36, 13:37
143. **The Last Supper V: The Way to the Father** Luke 22:35b, 22:36b-37, 22:38b, John 14:1-4, 14:5b, 14:6b-7, 14:8b, 14:9b-11, 14:12-14
144. **The Last Supper VI: Jesus Promises the Holy Spirit** John 14:15-17, 14:18-21,14:22b, 14:23-31a

145. **The Last Supper VII: The Greatest Love and The World's Hatred** John 15:1-17, 15:18-27
146. **The Last Supper VIII: Sadness Will Be Turned to Joy** John 16:1-13, 16:16, 16:17b-18, 16:19b-24, 16:32-33
147. **The Last Supper IX: The Prayer of Jesus** John 17:1-26
148. **The Garden of Gethsemane** Psalm 118:27-29, Matt 26:42, Mark 14:32b, 14:34b, 14:36b, 14:37b-38, 14:41b-42
149. **Jesus is Arrested** Matt 26:48b, 26:52b-54, Luke 22:48b, 22:49b, 22:52b-53, John 18:4b, 18:8
150. **Peter's First Denial** John 18:17b
151. **Jesus Before the High Council** Matt 26:61b, 26:62b, 26:63b, 26:68b, Mark 14:62b, 14:63b-64, John 18:20b-21, 18:22b, 18:23b
152. **Peter's Second and Third Denials** Matt 26:71b, 26:72b, 26:73b, 26:74b, 26:75b, John 18:26b
153. **Judas Hangs Himself** Matt 27:4b
154. **Jesus' Trial Before Pilate** Mark 15:4, Luke 23:4b, 23:5b, John 18:29b, 18:30a, 18:31a, 18:33b, 18:34b, 18:35b, 18:36b, 18:37b, 18:38a
155. **Jesus Sentenced to Death** Matt 27:19b, 27:21b, 27:22b, 27:24c, 27:25b, Mark 15:9a, Luke 23:14b-16, 23:18b, 23:22b, John 18:40b, John 19:4b, 19:6b, 19:7b, 19:10, 19:11b, 19:12b, 19:15
156. **The Crucifixion** Matt 27:40, 27:42-43, Luke 23:28b, 23:31, 23:34b, 23:39b, 23:40b-41, 23:42b, 23:43b, John 19:21b, 19:22b
157. **The Death of Jesus** Matt 27:49b, Mark 15:34b, 15:39b, John 19:26b, 19:27b
158. **The Sin-Bearing Messiah** Isaiah 53
159. **The Burial of Jesus** Matt 27:63b-64, 27:65b, John 19:36b-37
160. **The Resurrection** Matt 28:10c, Mark 16:3b, Luke 24:5b-7, John 20:18b
161. **The Cover Up** Matt 28:13b-14
162. **The Road to Emmaus** Luke 24:17b, 24:18b, 24:19b-24, 24:25b-26, 24:32b
163. **Jesus Appears to his Disciples** Luke 24:36b, 24:38b-39, 24:41b, 24:44b, 24:46b-48

164. **Doubting Thomas** John 20:25b, 20:27b, 20:28a, 20:29b
165. **Jesus Appears in Galilee** John 21:5b, 21:6b, 21:12a, 21:15, 21:16, 21:17
166. **The Great Commission** Matt 28:18b-20, Acts 1:4b-5, 1:6b, 1:7b-8, 1:11

About the Author

Carlee Yardley grew up in an evangelical Christian home. Her mum and dad, Daryl and Robyn Redford, led Young Life in Melbourne in the 70's, 80's and early 90's and Carlee saw hundreds of teenagers give their lives to Jesus over those years.

It wasn't until much later that Carlee realised that God has no grandchildren. It didn't matter how good her parents were at loving and discipling people, she knew she had to carve out her identity in Christ on her own. Carlee stripped back everything she knew about God and everything she knew about the church and started all over again from the gospels. In the process, this book was born.

Carlee's desire is that Christians everywhere will truly meet Jesus. Not the halo'ed Jesus the world portays, but the real Jesus of the Bible. The one full of love and forgiveness, who is tough on religious hypocrites and gracious enough to leave his throne to seek and save the lost.

Carlee is a primary school teacher and lives with her husband and four children near the sea in Coffs Harbour. She is happiest when she is surfing or skating with her family, or watching her two dogs wrestle.

www.ingramcontent.com/pod-product-compliance
Lightning Source LLC
Chambersburg PA
CBHW070135100426
42743CB00013B/2713